ALVIN ALEXSI CURRIER

SHADOWS OF YESTERDAY

Reflections from a life long search for the roots of Eastern European village life

*To Alice & Ron
Enjoy
Alvin Alexsi Currier*

Layout by Michael Riley
Photos by the author and Virgil Mlesnita

Dedicated to
Dumitru and Anuța Oaches,
their family,
and all the villagers of Ieud-Plopşor,
who are our relatives
through our spiritual roots
in the remaining Orthodox world.

Copyright © 2005 by
Alvin Alexsi Currier
(a.currier@juno.com)
All rights reserved
Printed in Canada
First edition

ISBN 978-0-9723411-1-0

Published by the author through
Light and Life Publishing Company
PO Box 26421,
Minneapolis, Minnesota.55426-0421
www.light-n-life.com

Acknowledgements

For these pages I am most indebted to the people all across Eastern Europe who over oh-so-many years, have opened to me their homes and their hearts, told me their stories, invited me to their weddings and feasts, allowed me to share their grief and joined with me in worship and prayer. If I listed the names of all who were my mentors, teachers, guides, translators, friends and encouragers, in Germany, America, Finland, Russia, Croatia and Romania, the list would be longer than the pages of this book. My gratitude and thanks goes out to all of you.

Especially I want to thank Michael Riley, who labored with me over many months with a combination of computer skills and personal patience, to achieve the graceful beauty that is the layout of this work.

The text is mine and most of the photos are mine, but because some of the best photos were taken by Virgil Mlesnita who often traveled with me in Romania, I want to particularly acknowledge him.

And, of course, a debt of gratitude is owed to my wife Anastasia, who always encouraged me, even though she so often lost her spouse to the mouse as I labored over the creation of these pages.

Doamne ajuta

May God preserve us.

Alvin Alexsi Currier

Alvin Alexsi Currier
Ajijic, Holy Pascha 2005

Foreword

A steeple is struck by the setting sun. It towers over a grassy meadow and in turn is dwarfed by the steep flank of the mountainside beyond, whose horizon conceals central Europe's great mountain wilderness: an area of icy streams and dense forests, the habitat of a few surviving wolf packs, of summer shepherd's encampments and of a scattering of remote monasteries. The steeple shimmers, light glancing off its hand-hewn shingles as if they were the scales of a darting Carpathian trout.

Welcome to the footnotes of a traveler. And to his footprints. And photographs. To his evocations of a world at once forever beyond our reach, and yet intimately made present.

As an Orthodox Christian pilgrim, Alexsi Currier has a common identity with the villagers of Romania's glorious Maramures. But it is his eye for spiritual treasure, and his empathy with a vast historic burden, that makes him build on this identity, and become something of incomparable value to any soul on a quest: a uniter of histories, a joiner of hearts, and encourager across great chasms between cultures.

To us, in this book he is an interpreter; to his friends in the village he is "Bunic", Grandpa. Haul out the rocker. There is a story to be told.

Jonathan Proctor
Doamne Ajuta
May God preserve us.

Chapter One: The Road Back

Chapter One:
The Road Back

In 1911, when my wife's grandmother left for America, she was seven months pregnant with the baby that would become Uncle Johnny. She came from the mountain ridge of Zumberak in what is today Croatia. She carried a passport of the Austrian Empire. She spoke Serbo-Croatian. With prepaid papers of passage, she traveled for six weeks, across Europe, the Atlantic Ocean and half way across the United States to join her husband. He had gone on ahead to earn the money for her journey by working in the mines by the little town of Chisholm, on the Mesabi iron range of northern Minnesota.

All together she bore seven children who grew and married, producing a second generation of grandchildren, followed by a third generation of great grandchildren. She died in the 1970's as the matriarch of a clan that numbered nearly a hundred. Over the many years of her life there were obviously occasional questions about where she came from. Sometimes she might answer by telling a tale or two before dismissing the subject. She always gave the impression that there was nothing to be gained by talking about where she came from. In her broken English she would state: "You American now. Is no good talk about the old country. Back there you are only hungry and working hard from before dawn to after dark. Is better to forget the old country. Is no need to ever go back there!"

She admonished us to "forget the old country,"

Chapter One: The Road Back

arguing that there is "no need to go back" but inevitably, as the generations of her descendants began to face the struggles of their own lives, they began to wonder about what made her such a commanding presence in all of our lives. What gave her the strength to carry the sufferings her life served her? What soil nurtured her fervent faith? Where did her compassion and humor come from? Inevitably we began to wonder about the old world that she came from. We began to wonder about the village life that formed her. We became curious about the forces that molded and made her. We felt a need to explore our peasant roots. This is how our journey to yesterday began. Little did we anticipate what awaited us.

Think of finding your roots as similar to opening an exotic Eastern European Matrushka or Nesting doll. You open the doll and, "Voila!" you discover another doll inside. You open that and you discover another, and so on and on. In looking for your roots you start by taking an interest in the place where your people came from. Open up that interest and you discover a history. Open up the history and you discover a culture. Open up the culture and you discover legends, tunes, songs, costumes, customs, architecture, embroidery and weaving. Open up any of these areas and you are confronted with a different way of life. You find yourself a hundred and fifty years ago in a land of horses, wagons, farms, fields, and forests. Enter into the experience of this way of life and you begin to discover

yourself thinking in a different way. Open yourself up to that different way of thinking, and only then do you begin to reach the heart of the world that is the village.

It may begin with a seemingly inconsequential curiosity, but it seldom ends that way.

Years ago when I was a college Chaplain, a young girl eagerly sought me out at the end of the summer vacation. During the vacation she had traveled to Greece. Her grandparents had come from Greece. In the spring, as she was planning the trip, she had confided in me that she wanted to visit the village of her grandparents. Her parents discouraged her from traveling alone so far up into the remote mountains of northern Greece. She asked my advice. I encouraged her. When she returned this is the story she had to tell:

"After getting off the bus I spent most of the morning trudging up a dusty, winding, dirt road, past isolated farmhouses, until in the blazing noonday sun the cluster of squat blindingly white buildings that made up the village appeared. I lost all my courage. I had to force myself to move. I couldn't see a soul. I finally made it right into the midst of the buildings and only then did a young man about my age appear. In astonishment he studied me, my little backpack, and my western clothes. He addressed me with a blast of Greek. His eyes widened as he realized that I didn't speak Greek. I pointed a finger at myself and announced the name of my grandparents. Again his eyes widened even further in astonishment. He repeated my grandparents name in a voice that sounded like a thunderclap. In a sudden flood of Greek, punctuated with the repeated mentions of my grandparents' name, he indicated that I was to wait right there. He ran away. I stood in the middle of the road in the middle of the village. Curious villagers began to appear, at a distance, but in a circle all around me. I could hear a murmur of conversation.

"I stood there and waited and waited. I was terrified. I wanted to cry. I wanted to faint but I couldn't. Then, at the far end of the street, a dozen or so people appeared with the young man. I can't describe them all but in the center was an old man in a wrinkled suit. He was obviously an important person. His face was weathered and his eyes were intense. He walked right up to me and the crowd folded in around me. He spoke in a commanding voice and from somewhere an English translation appeared.

I showed him my passport and explained to the translator that my grandparents had come from this village. A great buzz of excitement passed through the crowd. He asked my grandfather's name and when I answered there were gasps. When he asked about my grandmother it was the same, but when he asked about my father and mother my answers were met with stony silence. Next the old man walked to within inches of my face, and spoke in short strong sentences of Greek that hit me in translation as follows:

"Your grandfather and your grandmother were born in this village." He took a long pause before saying deliberately and emphatically: "But they left this village and never came back." It seemed to me that he shouted the words *never came back*. His flashing eyes stared at me as he continued. "Your father was born to a father and to a mother that came from this village, but he never came back." Again he seemed to shout the last words: *never came back*.

Then everything happened all at once. He started to speak again. His voice was low and soft. I heard a murmur in the crowd. People started to cross themselves. Then a wailing began. I was terrified. Then I

Chapter One: The Road Back

noticed that the old man's eyes were filled with tears. The English translation drifted into my consciousness as he embraced me and kissed me on both cheeks.

"But you, my child, you have come back, you have come back, we are your family, this is your village, this is your home, you belong here, welcome, welcome, welcome home."

The young woman ended her story with vivid vignettes of the days that followed as she experienced the village that would now be hers forever.

My wife and I had a similar experience when we met Donald Marinkovic in the 1980s. The parents of Mr. Marinkovic came from the village of Osunja located (or lost) high on the Zumberak mountain in Croatia. In America, after his father died, Donald's mother ran a boarding house up on the Iron Range of northern Minnesota. Donald grew up fluent in the Zumberak mountain dialect and filled with village lore. Because we knew the Zumberak area, I agreed to visit his family's village and arrange a visit for him. I walked a whole day through the high mountain meadows and forest groves to reach Osunja. The cemetery I passed just outside the village was full of graves bearing the name of Marinkovic. The village seemed deserted. Finally, I startled an old lady shelling peas on the shady side of her house. With my few words of the language I managed to stammer something to the effect that I was an American and I had a friend whose name was Marinkovic. Suddenly a crowd appeared, all chattering

at the same time. The seemingly deserted village had hidden a multitude of eyes that had followed me through shutter slats and door cracks. I was led to a home where a senior Marinkovic appeared and I managed to communicate with my few words and a lot of charades that I would return next fall with this Mr. Marinkovic from America.

Months later in America when the travel arrangements had been made I pasted a picture of Donald Marinkovic on a 4x6 card, wrote his name underneath, pasted my picture next to his, to identify who was writing, and with words from the dictionary I announced that we would come to the village on Saturday October 17th 1987. I put the card in an envelope, addressed it to the senior Marinkovic, and mailed it off to Europe.

With great formality the Osunja Marinkovic welcomed the American Marinkovic. Suddenly there was a great burst of laughter and the two men fell into each others arms kissing and crying. Evidently the welcoming man had just said that there was no longer any doubt that they were related, because no one else in the world had such big noses like they had. There followed a day of feasting and visits around that village that left us all dazed, amazed, and exhausted.

After traveling with a tour to Europe that autumn, my wife and I drove to what was then Yugoslavia and met Donald Marinkovic at the Zagreb airport. With our rental car we left Zagreb early in the morning of Saturday the 17th. In low gear on a narrow road of switch back curves, we slowly made our ascent up onto the mountain of Zumberak. There the road evaporated into a one lane dirt track. Nearing midday we bumped over a rise on a road through a field and the village came into view. We bounced down into the huddle of houses and pulled up in front of the weathered, senior Marinkovic home. To our astonishment the whole village was waiting for us. People came from everywhere calling to each other the announcement of our arrival. The whole village encircled our car. Then slowly the door of the house opened and a proud middle aged man came out tugging on his worn leather vest that was now too small for his middle. Donald got out of the car and stood watching as his distant relative approached.

Chapter One: The Road Back

These stories of discovering roots now span over fifty years and they pretty well parallel and portray the story of my own life. For an academic year in Scotland, I first traveled to Europe as a student. Freshly ordained, I served country churches on the prairies of Minnesota. As an American exchange pastor, I spent time in the Black Forest of Germany. Eleven years as a college Chaplain allowed me to travel regularly to Europe from 1964 to 1975. Thereafter I found myself living without electricity in the log cabin of a forested religious retreat in Wisconsin. By the late seventies my search for spiritual roots had opened me to the ancient Eastern Orthodox Churches. Spurred by my experience in the forest and consumed by a fascination with the old ways still

traceable in Eastern Orthodox Finland, I managed for nearly twenty years to keep traveling there. As the Soviet Union began to crumble I went there to witness my Russian friends attempt to find their past which had been so brutally crushed by 70 years of Communism. In the early eighties when my wife went back to Yugoslavia to find the villages that her grandparents came from, we discovered for the first time an area so isolated that they were still rooted in the traditional peasant ways of subsistence farming.

So it was that slowly over the span of half a century the insights and convictions that follow took form. They grew out of rich first-hand experiences and the research that such experiences inspired. They had no

Chapter One: The Road Back

information our immigrant forebearers passed on about the old country was not only very sketchy, but it was often notoriously inaccurate. There are many reasons for this.

The most obvious reason was the ebb and flow of history. Especially in Eastern Europe, the borders often changed in the matter of just a few years. A hundred years ago, the border between Austria and Russia existed deep inside what is today the Ukraine. A hundred years ago Poland, as a nation, didn't exist at all.

In a book about Eastern Europe the following quote is found. "In his lifetime my grandfather saw many lands. He was born in the Austrian-Hungarian Empire. He grew up in Czechoslovakia. Later he lived

logical order nor can I order them logically. Instead, like climbing a mountain, they combined to grant an ever broader and richer view. Sometimes, like reaching a knoll on an alpine ascent, there was a moment of awe and inspiration as a whole new perspective opened up. To this day the journey continues.

As we will see, especially if your ancestors were from Eastern Europe and you have the actual present-day name and location of the place they came from, then you are among the rare and lucky few. In most cases, the task of finding an actual place isn't as easy as it was in the case of the young Greek woman. It is common knowledge among any who have sought to find their actual ancestral village that often whatever in Hungary. For many years he lived in the Soviet Union. At his life's end he died and was buried in the Ukraine, or to be precise in the town of Mukacevo where he was born and which he never left throughout his whole life."

Sometimes when the borders and rulers changed, people were driven from their villages and sometimes they were simply or forcibly absorbed into the culture of the new rulers. I once took two American boys to Austria to visit the village where their grandfather was born and raised. The boy's family was proud of being Austrian. When we arrived at the ancestral home we quickly discovered that their roots were not Austrian at all, but solidly Slovenian. The boys were Slavs and not Germans. The area has been annexed by Austria and over less than a century the Slovenian language and culture had been all but totally replaced by the German language and Austrian culture.

From these lands with such fluid borders, people speaking many different tongues arrived in America traveling with passports of the Austro-Hungarian or Russian Empire. Is it any wonder then that the descendants of these Eastern European immigrants might have confused stories about whom they are and the location of the ancestral village?

In the case of my wife's grandmother our search was helped by three extremely wise questions that were posed by my wife's aunt. As the last of the generation

Chapter One: The Road Back

that had come from the Old Country were aging, she asked one of them, first of all, if he could tell her what land he came from and what it is called today. He answered, "Back then it was Austria, but today it is called Yugoslavia." Next she asked if he could remember the closest big town. This time he answered, "Well back then it was called Agram, but today it is called Zagreb." Lastly she asked the final and most clever question. "If you were in Zagreb and wanted to go home, which direction would you go and how long would it take you? To this the old man replied, "I 'd go due west to Sonnenberg and then it would take me five hours to walk up the mountain." With this information it wasn't hard to locate the present day Samobor that is the Croatian name of the Austrian town, which in German was Sonnenberg. The mountain rising above Samobor is called the Zumberak Mountain. We already knew the name of the village and the fact that it was in Zumberak, so once we found the mountain, we easily located the village itself.

Obviously the fluctuating boundaries and rapidly changing national names were a major factor in the notorious inaccuracy with which so many of our immigrant ancestors described where they came from. However I am convinced that there is another, even more fundamental, reason for their inability to explain where they came from. This deeper reason is to be found in the very nature of the place they came from.

They came from the village. They came from a different way of thinking. They came from a different world.

In speaking of how the village perceives itself, the Romanian scholar Lucian Blaga, puts it this way: "The village is not located in a purely material geography, somewhere upon the grid of mechanical space coordinates, as the city is; to its awareness of itself, the village lies at the center of the world and extends into myth. The village is integrated in a cosmic destiny, in an all-inclusive life span, beyond which nothing exists anymore. This is the latent consciousness of the village, its own awareness of itself."

To a villager, in his consciousness, the village is the center of the world. To a villager the measure of the

known world is essentially the surrounding area that is within walking distance. The mountain meadows where the sheep are taken for the summer and the distant forests where timber and firewood are cut; these places, like some towns, are extensions of the known world around the village. Everything beyond is almost equally unknown. Budapest and Bucharest are as unimaginable as Beijing or Baltimore.

The other side of understanding the village as the center of the world is the fact that anyplace that can't easily be reached from the village becomes necessarily nebulous. Beyond the border of the known world begins the unknown world. For our ancestors, the journey to America was like a trip through outer space.

Chapter One: The Road Back

 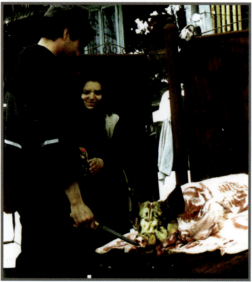 

They left the bright star that was their village at the center of their universe. It faded fast as they traveled past thousands of other villages, towns, cities, countries, lands, and across the ocean. They lost their point of reference. How did you explain to someone in Minnesota where Raditzina by Drohobych is? It was out there, like one of the millions of stars in the night sky. Somewhere back there was their planet, with their land, with their valley and with their familiar hills. Somewhere back there was their world with their village at the center of it. They knew that, but they lost track of how to find their way back. The space between where they found themselves now and the place that they came from, was as mysterious as the vast heavens of the night sky above them.

Although it is true to say that an unknown world surrounded the known world of the village, in another sense this unknown world was not unknown at all. As Lucian Blaga says: "the village lies at the center of the world and extends into myth." This mythological realm surrounding the village was vitally alive. It was filled with dangers and demons as well as angels and archangels. It stretched from the village beyond the geography of earth into realms of heaven and hell. In it dwelt God. In it lurked the Devil. In this realm, America existed on the same plane with the mansions in the sky that the Savior had promised the faithful. This world beyond the village was both terrifying and luring.

The role of what was known about the unknown is vividly reflected in the drama that surrounded the return of the young Greek girl to the village of her grandparents. Like Odysseus returning to Ithaca in Homer's Odyssey, the young girl returned from a place the villagers couldn't imagine. America? America? America was to the villagers a mythological place, known to them only through rumors, word of mouth, and occasional letters. To them the world beyond the village is still the same place of terror and temptation that Odysseus journeyed through. This is the reason for the overflowing emotion that surrounded the fact that she finally found her way home.

So just as America had once existed in a mythological space for so many of our immigrant ancestors, now in America their old country village existed only in their memory. It was like a dream or a fairy tale. It existed as a mythological place and so it remained as the years passed and children grew to be parents, and then grandchildren and great grandchildren were born. So it remained until according to the strange chemistry of families, clans and tribes, someone became curious about where they came from. So it remained until someone wanted to better understand their roots.

Today, if you can find the actual name of the place that your ancestors came from, it is possible to visit that place. In the last decades of the 20th, century the Iron Curtain has melted away and all of Eastern Europe is

Chapter One: The Road Back

now accessible. Visas may be expensive and the roads may be full of potholes, but travel is possible. However, what you will discover is that not only is travel possible for us but it is also possible for everyone else. Peddlers and merchants, gurus and missionaries are pouring into these former Communist countries. Cast off clothes come by the container load to the markets. Coca Cola trucks crawl along even the roughest of roads. Cars full of curious tourists weave between the local horse carts.

And if you visit Eastern Europe today, you will discover not only that the outsiders are coming in, but you will also see that the villagers are going out. Everyday cars and busses depart from Poland and Romania headed for farm work and construction jobs in Western Europe. This process spells doom for the isolated villages that are still rooted in the old way of life. An era is ending. The mythological world surrounding the village evaporates as the village girls take jobs as domestics in posh Italian and Swiss homes, and the calloused hands from the village fields find jobs in the West that pay in Euros. With a certain disappointment you may find that today the place that your ancestors came from, has become little more than an Eastern European edition of the fast food chains, fashion clothes, flashy cars and super markets that we know as a way of life in America.

The times have changed and are changing. Today, to explore, to sense, to feel, and to experience the world

Shadows of Yesterday

your forebears left, you most likely will have to pass beyond the actual village of their birth to search out the genre of village that bred them. You will have to move out into the marshes along the Polish-Belorussian border, or into the vast dense forests of the North, or perhaps into the high isolated valleys of the Carpathian Mountains. Only here in these remote regions can one still today find people living in the world of the village as they have for centuries. In my own quest, after over fifty years of digging ever deeper to find the village roots of Western and European Christian culture, it was at a monastery high up in the Carpathians that a young novice gave me the gift that would lead me finally to what was to become my village.

Chapter Two: My Village

Chapter Two: My Village

The Feast of the Annunciation celebrates the angel Gabriel's announcement to the Virgin Mary that she will conceive and bear a son. Logically this feast falls exactly nine months before the birth. On the eve of March 25th, 1998, I arrived with an American Deacon of the Orthodox Church at the Monastery of Saint Ann, located high in the Carpathian Mountains near the Romanian village of Rohia. It was cold up there. We were in the clouds. There was a luminescence more than a light. Snowflakes drifted between the shadowy trees. We were warmly welcomed by a monk who showed us around the monastery, and then while standing on a walkway catching fleeting glimpses of the surrounding peaks through the swirling luminosity, he proceeded to tell us a most incredible story of how the monastery came to be built so high up in the mountains.

Leaning on the railing, he matter-of-factly related how back in the early 1920s the young daughter of the village priest had died and then returned to her father in a dream on three consecutive nights to beg him to build a monastery. With struggles, the grieving father had found the money to buy a piece of land. He erected and blessed a wooden cross to mark the land, but the cross soon disappeared. A long time later a woodcutter found the cross high up on the mountain. The cross was then returned to the purchased land and an old shepherd volunteered to guard it. That night it

Chapter Two: My Village

snowed and when the morning came the cross was gone but there were no footprints in the snow. Again the cross was found on top of the mountain, and this time everyone realized that the angels had moved it to mark where the monastery was to be built. Our monastic host ended his story by saying simply: "and that's how the monastery came to be on top of the mountain."

The following morning the Divine Liturgy for the Feast of the Annunciation was celebrated at an elaborate outside altar, and the incredible story of the founding of the monastery was followed by an equally incredible witness of fervent faith. The closest town was miles away, and yet, slowly out of the mist of the dawn, hundreds of people of all ages emerged from the steep forest paths to stand and kneel in the snow for the service. The service lasted three hours. It was freezing cold.

Finally, nearing sundown on this memorable day, our host walked us out along the mountaintop toward the cow barn to show us the crumbling remains of a hut where a sainted hermit had once lived. While we were there, we also took a look in the barn. Inside there were two young novices who had the monastic duty or obedience of tending the cattle. They warily watched us as we looked around. When we left the barn, the others hurried back for the Vespers service but I stayed on with the interpreter to photograph the old hermitage. Again the incredible happened. As I came down the hill that I had climbed to take the picture, I noticed that one of the novices was approaching us. He advanced timidly, as if every step cost him great effort. He carried in his hands, held out before him, one of the beautiful traditional black sheepskin vests of the area. Shyly he informed the interpreter that his mother had made the vest and he would like to give it to me as a gift. I was overwhelmed. I had long admired and coveted just such a vest. Now it was simply given to me as a gift.

As this amazing feast day ended, I dimly sensed that something had happened. As our ancestors had once left the world of the village to travel to what was then called the New World, so today I had entered a realm beyond the familiar logic, rationalism, and skepticism, of the modern western world. With an implausible miracle story, an inconceivable witness of passionate faith, and a simple gesture of unimaginable generosity, my intuition told me that I had crossed a threshold. I had found a portal into the world of the village. It still existed. It was open before me. I couldn't imagine what was ahead and I couldn't wait to find out.

Actually the vest fit snugly. I had received it reverently, immediately tried it on, and then posed for a

Chapter Two: My Village

picture with the novice who had given it to me. He had asked me to send a copy of the picture, to his parents in the village, so I copied down the address. A couple of days later the idea dawned on me to try to find the novice's mother and ask her if I could pay her to make a larger vest, purportedly for a friend of mine. In this way I arrived at that fateful day when I first drove to the village.

If you look on the map you can find the place that I am writing about. It is a high valley folded into the western slope of the Carpathian Mountains along the Ukrainian border. To the north the rugged Carpathian peaks rise up into the Ukraine. To the east there is only one treacherous pass over the same peaks down into Romanian Moldavia. To the south a line of heavily forested mountainous ridges creates a final challenging natural border. These ridges force the three rivers draining this basin to flow northwest for some sixty miles before spilling down into the Hungarian plain. The hidden valley that they hollow out is called the land of Maramures. Although the first settlers arrived in this hidden valley over a thousand years ago, this land of Maramures has always remained uniquely isolated. Even today there are only six roads into this area, and each one of them winds around switchbacks to crawl over a pass through the mountains. Until late in the last century, these ways were little more than well worn and rutted wagon trails. Electricity did not reach

Chapter Two: My Village

the Maramures villages until the 1990s.

The address that the novice had given me was easy to find. Most of the villages in the valley grew up along one of the main rivers or along one of the creeks that flowed down into a river. I turned off the main road that followed the river, and drove along a creek on a once tarred road that was now sorely potholed. Occasional homesteads hugged the road. I drove past pecking chickens and playing children. I drove past horse drawn wagons loaded with logs, hay, or persons. I wove between individuals and groups of people walking. After two miles, the houses clustered along the way thickened to surround the center of the village with it's enormous new cement Church, a village hall, a school, a bar, a single store and the mayor's office. I continued on. The village thinned. Small fields reappeared between the homesteads. The road turned to gravel. Slowly over another two miles, it narrowed into a rutted way of earth that lead to the last houses and fields nestled in the hollow of the surrounding forested hills. Finally I arrived at the family home of the novice. It stood tight up to the road, enclosed by a wooden fence just high enough for privacy, yet low enough to talk over. It had an elaborately carved gateway with massive doors for wagons to pass through and a smaller door for people. I had driven maybe four miles and arrived one hundred and fifty years ago.

I parked in front of what might be called a homestead, a peasant's cottage, or a small farm, but actually there is no English word that adequately portrays the place. Depending on the prosperity of the family, it is a smaller or larger compound of buildings or sheds surrounding a yard. It has a house for the humans, a stall for the horse or horses and another for the cow or cows. It has a shed for the wood and a shed for the wagon, a hutch for the rabbits and a pen for the pig. Birds roost in the rafters and cats prowl in the shadows. The yard is busy with chickens, ducks or geese, and a guard dog is chained in the corner. Usually a fence encircles this compound to keep the inhabitants in and the predators out. Surrounding the yard is an orchard of apple, plum and nut trees, a massive vegetable garden, and the fields of potatoes, corn and grains.

But a village home is also much more than just the physical buildings and the fields surrounding it. It is a space alive with life. It is an organism yielding the minimal needs for human survival in exchange for the labor of constant care and tending. It is the classroom and workshop where values and skills are learned. It is the treasury where the memorials from the departed are kept. It is the locus of birth and death. It is the sanctuary where baptisms, engagements, weddings, funerals and feast days are celebrated. It is the stage on which life is played out. It is the heart of the peasant's world. Few ever travel far from it.

In the complex village understanding of reality, each peasant home has its own aura of sovereignty. It is the realm and domain of the family. In the kingdom that is the village, it has its own name, position and status. It is the bastion of family honor, the locus of a visceral loyalty, and in the local lore and legends it has its own unique history.

A well woven story will tell of its settlement perhaps in the times of some King, or under the protection of this or that Duke. The history will list the family heroes like the great grandfather who helped to build the Church, or the distant uncle who severed the head of the Sultan in a great battle with the Turks. It will detail how the grandfather built the house, which bedroom the father was born in and where an aunt wasted away

to her death when she was only ten years old. It will delight in embellishing everything humorous, such as the story of how one spring morning Grandma grabbed a broom stick and ran outside through the mushy snow in her nightgown to drive away the bear that was trying to get the pig. In the village every home is intimately known.

Peasant life plays itself out in the kitchen. At this home of the novice, the kitchen was a small outbuilding dominated by a massive stone stove. Only the immediate family is allowed in this space. Guests here as everywhere are always received in the finest room on the farm set aside, as far as the family means allow, for special occasions. I was therefore ushered into a formal

Chapter Two: My Village

room which was in the two-room family house. It took my breath away. It was an art gallery. It was an exhibit of treasures. It was a display of weaving, from bright flowered woolen rugs hung on the wall to patterned ceremonial towels draped over the icons, from heavy woolen blankets to fine linen bedding. It was a display of embroidery, from the bouquets of the pillows piled on the bed to the tablecloth covering the corner table. It was a room alive with handwork masterpieces.

    Here hospitality was lavished on me. Jumping over the little fence that kept the chickens out of the flowers around the little house, the daughters now started to appear with food from the kitchen. The father of the family came in from the field, grabbed a bottle of spirits from his own still, and poured welcoming glasses of "white lightning." Outside, a chicken squawked its last, and in due course after breads, cheeses and sausages, appeared on the table as dinner.
In response to my request, the traditional festive costumes were taken out of the cupboard and the girls dressed in their elaborate blouses, flowered skirts and thick woolen aprons woven in the colors and patterns that marked their village.

    As the sun sank behind the hills, plodding horses began to pass by pulling wagonloads of tired men and women homeward after a long day of labor cutting wood in the forest, hoeing in the fields or scything in distant meadows. It came time for me to leave. I

was loaded down with gifts, including by the way, a larger vest.

I wove my way back out of the village past horses and wagons, past groups of people walking, some with scythes over their shoulders, past the chickens still pecking, the children still playing and the elders now visiting away on their benches. I headed toward a world across the ocean that these villagers could little imagine. For the most part the only world they knew was right here. They had everything they needed for the only way of life they knew. They raised their own food, built their own houses and made their own clothes. Their life was hard work but it wasn't all hard work. It was rich with festivals and celebrations. It was rich with families, caring, and faith. It was rich with traditional costumes, customs, music and dance. I knew that I would be back. It was a place of fascinating, intriguing riches, a place rich in almost everything except that one thing by which so much of the rest of the world has come to measure wealth. Most of the villagers had little or no money. Most of them were dirt poor. ❧

Chapter Three: Discovering the Village World

Chapter Three: Discovering the Village World

What is wealth? What is poverty? Contact with the village calls forth questions such as these. It can be like following Alice through the looking glass into Wonderland. So much seems upside down from the way that we have been accustomed to it. In the village wealth isn't a matter of money. Villagers are very rich on a very low cash flow. Poverty is often a matter of not having the things that money can't buy, like health, a spouse, children or peace of mind.

A while back I discovered the low carbohydrate diet and trimmed off 25 pounds. I was delighted and sent off a photo of the new me to the village in Romania. Almost immediately I received a moving letter almost begging me to come and live in the village. "You will always be our grandfather," the letter vowed, "and we will love and take care of you." I couldn't figure out this sudden solicitousness. I politely refused. One evening months later when I returned to the village, I finally inquired about the letter. Then it was explained to me that when the people had seen that picture of me they had all become concerned about my health. Obviously I had lost a lot of weight so I must be sick. They wanted to take care of me. They wanted to fatten me up to my old self again.

Gradually, through incidents such as this, certain awarenesses and insights started to crystallize in my consciousness. An idea of how the village views itself and its world began to take shape. It was a slow proc-

Chapter Three: Discovering the Village World

ess. I tested every observation. Some were simple and sort of humorous, like observing that in America fat is out and trim is in. Others were more complex. Is the distance to the village chronological as well as geographical? Did I fly a few thousand miles, drive four miles up a valley, and arrive at a place one hundred and fifty years ago? I asked myself what difference it might make that they are intimate with agriculture and animals while we are intimate with electronics and cyberspace. I pondered that our emphasis tends toward the individual and freedom while theirs leans toward the tradition of the community. I wondered if we are poor in what they are rich in, and they are poor in what we weigh as wealth. Very slowly I struggled to understand from the inside the hidden place where I had landed.

In terms of geography as we know it, the world of the village is very small. Its outside boundary is essentially set by the distance one can cover in a day by walking from the center. But villagers do not understand their world in terms of geography. They have no concept of geography. The physical area of the village might be miniscule by our measure but it is a space vibrantly alive with energies we moderns can hardly imagine. It is teaming with benevolent and malevolent forces and beings. Curses, charms and prayers electrify the air. Writing from his childhood memories, the Romanian scholar Lucian Blaga put it this way: "There was the village, built on purpose around the Church

and graveyard, that is, around God and the dead. The arrangement was like an undertone lending to the whole a touch of indispensable mystery. I would place God in the ritual space behind the iconostasis, whence I could sense Him irradiating upon the world. That was not a story, told to me like many others, but an unshakable belief."

In contrast to this village view, our western world embraces a geography that includes the whole earth and expands into interstellar space, but except for a few floaters of faith, philosophy or ideology, this vast area is relatively empty of any compelling unifying convictions.

Perhaps the most profound awareness that slowly took form from my experiences was the childlikeness of the village world. Not only is the developmental level of the village some one hundred and fifty years distant, but their way of viewing reality and reacting to each other exists untouched by anything like our modern psychology or social science. Village life exhibits a raw humanness that predates modification by the likes of sensitivity training or communication skills. It exists in a prescientific age. It is potent with fervent faith and virile prejudices. It is both horribly and delightfully childlike. As with children, I have often watched in horror the total unleashing of emotions, complete with contorted facial expressions, bulging blood vessels and screaming language, followed in a relatively short time

Chapter Three: Discovering the Village World

by a restoration of friendship as if nothing at all had ever happened. On the other hand I have often been delighted in being a part of the childlike abandon with which villagers give themselves to celebration, hospitality and gratitude.

A village boy was once injured by a falling tree. His recovery forced him to spend some weeks far from his home in the hospital of the provincial town. During his stay there a distant friend who lived in the town faithfully visited the lonely boy. After the injured boy was released, nothing was heard from him for weeks until 8:30 one morning in the week before Easter. A knock came on the door of the friend in town. When the startled family opened the door, the boy from the village stood there with a little lamb folded in his arms. The village boy had left at 5:30 in the morning to walk six kilometers to catch the bus over the mountain to the provincial town to bring this family an Easter lamb as a token of his gratitude.

It is fascinating to explore the world of the village because the village is the world of our roots. Yet a danger lurks in this adventure. It is easy to lose our sense of balance. It is tempting to wax eloquent about the simple life, to read Henry David Thoreau, and to imagine the village like the set for Fiddler on the Roof. But Thoreau only lived a couple of years at Walden Pond, and the reality of the Jewish Shtetl was a lot different from the costumes and color of the stage or screen set.

Years ago when my writing verged on idealizing

the old Finnish tribes, Senni Timonen, the respected scholar of Finnish folklore, warned me of the danger, and implored me to avoid the trap, of romanticism. She pointed out that without a doubt the song singers of those vast northern forests possessed a treasure. But it was in their memory and singing. Physically they often existed near starvation in chimneyless log huts, through bitter cold winters and nearly endless darkness. Certainly the physical poverty of many of our ancestors was similar. In one of his novels, Joseph Roth describes conditions in a poor village with these words: "Living became dearer from year to year. The crops were always poorer and poorer. The carrots diminished, the eggs were hollow, the potatoes froze, the soup was watery, the carp thin, the pike short, the ducks lean, the geese tough, and the chickens amounted to nothing."

We must never lose sight of the fact that at this lowest level there is in the villages this kind of devastating, debilitating and destructive poverty. In the past it was more pervading but it still exists today. It is the slow loss in the struggle for hope, health, heart and soul. This reality forever forbids any romantic illusions.

Yet most of village life, in the past as well as today, exists just a tad above this lowest level of desperation. It exists at a level of endless hard labor that yields just enough to supply and satisfy both body and soul. It is a life bound up with the earth. Exhausting hours of daily chores return with every dawn: milk the cow, feed the stock, clean the stalls, chop the wood, cook the meals. Moons wax and wane through the seasons beckoning now to sow, now to reap, now to scythe the hay and now to fell the trees for winter fires. The cycle is never ending, so the villager forms it into routines and rituals. Tradition emerges. Tradition is at the heart of village life. Tradition is the way the villager relates to the world.

It is like the path over the mountain to the next village. Other trails may look shorter, more level, or safer, but over the years they have been found to hide gullies, cliffs or other pitfalls. It is believed that if a better path had existed, it would have been found. The villager trusts the path that is worn. It is accepted that the fabric of village life is woven on the warp and woof of the grueling routines and rituals of the peasant farm. But these routines and rituals are not mechanical and predictable. They are unpredictable. They are bound up with the earth.

As Peter Berger writes: "Each day a peasant experiences more change more closely than any other class. Some of these changes, like those of the seasons or like the process of ageing and failing energy, are fore-

Chapter Three: Discovering the Village World

seeable; many – like the weather from one day to the next, like a cow choking to death on a potato, like lightening, like rains which come too early or too late, like fog that kills the blossom, like … an epidemic, like locusts – are unpredictable."

The forces of nature are palpable in peasant life. Nature's blessings, beauty and bounty, as well as her caprice and fury, are intimately experienced. The human mind struggles to bring order and understanding to this chaos of experiences. Out of this struggle emerge the fundamental religious convictions of the village world.

The English word *religion* is created out of the Latin root *ligare* and the Latin prefix *re*. The Latin verb, *ligare* means to tie, bind, or bundle things together. It is the same root that is behind the English word, *ligament*. Here it refers to the belief system that holds or binds a people together. But the word religion has the Latin prefix *re* which means *back*. Together *re* and *ligare* form the word *religion* which now means the tradition or the traditions that tie back, repeat, and reinforce the beliefs of a people. Religion is therefore the beliefs of a people and the traditions through which those beliefs are transmitted and celebrated.

On the darker side, there are beliefs and traditions birthed and fed by fear or desire. The village world exists far before anything like psychology. Demons, ghosts and witches account for the unexplainable. Curses cause the cow to lose her milk. Mirrors are turned to the wall when somebody dies. Charms cause the selected suitor to be attracted. Potions help the wife to conceive. Wedding greenery is kept to guarantee good luck by being boiled into the water for the first bath of the first born. The sign of the cross protects.

One autumn afternoon we went up the mountain to bless a cross. It was a Sunday. After liturgy in the morning and a leisurely meal over the noon hour, a call from the road summoned us to come along and climb into the wagon. Further along the road, the priest, his wife and the young cantor climbed in. We were 16 persons in our wagon, and another loaded wagon followed us. The horses strained to pull us. As we entered the forest, the road evaporated into a rut-

ted trail.

The cross that we were heading to bless stood ahead in a small clearing about three kilometers beyond the last houses of the village. Beside it, a little spring flowed into a trough for travelers and their animals to drink from. Decades ago a pious villager had erected a cross in the clearing to shelter those who rested there, for the forest is filled with fear for the villagers. It marks the end of their known world. In it dwell not only wild animals but also unpredictable and malevolent spirits. At one point as we rocked along, everyone in the cart crossed themselves. It was explained to me that at this point in the winter twelve years ago a load of logs had slid or been pulled off the icy path and cast down into the creek below. Four men and a horse had perished.

Over the years the cross had rotted and weathered until those who passed it began to worry about it. There had been accidents in the forest. Men cutting timber had been struck by falling trees. Others had slipped, stumbled or fallen and broken bones. Wolves had attacked passing sheep. It was obviously time to have the cross repaired and repainted. One family undertook the cause.

Now we had come to bless it anew. With incense, holy water and prayers, the refurbishing was solemnly finished. Now again the clearing would be a safe haven for anyone resting here. It would protect those who must labor deeper in the wooded darkness. With new power it would defend the village below from any evil that might attempt to descend into it. Everyone breathed a sigh of relief. Blankets were cast on the ground, baskets of food emerged, and the schnapps bottles were opened. Clinking glasses sealed the ceremony with toasts that proclaimed: "God be blessed!" and "Blessed be God!"

Although dark forms still lurk around the fringe of the village, the roots of religious life are secured deep in the soil of the Church. She is the interior world that orders and explains the external struggle for subsistence survival. She is at the heart of the world of the village, both literally and figuratively. The old Church on the knoll in the center of the village dates from 1364. It has been built and rebuilt over more than six centuries. The

Chapter Three: Discovering the Village World

weathered wooden structure that stands there today is already over two centuries old. Around it circles the cemetery. Many graves date back beyond all records. According to tradition, the whole village gathers every autumn to clean and decorate the graves, light candles and observe the service of memorial prayers for the departed. Since time immemorial it was so.

To an outsider, the villagers are Christians of the Eastern or Orthodox tradition. To understand what this means, we must wade a little way out into the sea of Church history. This is no simple matter for strong tides, currents and undertows course in these waters. I believe that most would agree that for the first thousand years of the Christian faith the Church was one. It was during this first millennium of Christianity that the theology of the faith was defined, and a relatively common tradition of worship and practice evolved. In the predominantly Greek-speaking East, the Church was centered in the ancient mother Churches of Jerusalem, Alexandria, Antioch and Constantinople. The Latin speaking Western Church was centered in Rome.

Slowly, differences developed between Rome and the Eastern jurisdictions of the Church. Finally a split came, and as it deepened, the once common tradition of religious worship and practice began to reflect the divergence. In the ninth century, when two Greek missionaries, Cyril and Methodius, created a written language for the Slavs, translating the texts and traditions of the faith into the language of that people, they encountered severe opposition from some of the Western

Bishops. In the Western Church, Latin became the language of worship, administration and scholarship while the Eastern Churches held to the belief that the faith should always be preached and practiced in the language of the people. In the West the clergy were called to celibacy, while in the East they continued to marry.

In the West three dimensional images, or statutes, appeared, while the East continued to argue that only two dimensional images, or iconographic paintings, should be allowed. Essentially the Eastern Churches remained conservative, holding strictly to the inherited traditions, while in the Western Church the tradition continued to evolve. The western Christians came to be known as the Roman Catholic Church, while those remaining in the Eastern regions called themselves "Orthodox," which means the "right or correct worshipping ones."

It is my conviction that, as the divergence widened, a subtle but important shift in emphasis appeared. Orthodoxy tended to continue to express the faith primarily through the heart, while the Western Church awakened to also approaching the faith with the mind. Orthodoxy tended to withdraw into its trusted tradition, while Catholicism wrestled to reconcile both the faith and tradition with the intellect. Subjecting their tradition to the scrutiny of reason, the Western Church not only generated great theology, scholarship and renewal, but it also spawned the Reformation, the proliferation of Protestantism, and today's plethora of evangelical mega-churches. While the storms of the Renaissance, the Reformation and the Enlightenment swept over the Western Christians, Orthodoxy faithfully continued on in the hallowed traditions of the first millennium of the faith. Indeed it is hard to imagine a distance greater than that which evolved between the vast span of modern Western Christianity and the ancient Churches of Orthodoxy.

That distance is reflected in the way the villagers and the Orthodox view themselves. They do not understand their religious life in the academic way that I have just explained it. They do not stand outside of it, viewing it as a line of historical names, dates and places stretching across two thousand years. Their religious life is a circle that they exist inside of. It is the cycle of feasts and fasts, births and burials, seedtime and harvest. It is the tradition that is, has, and ever will be. They do not analyze it, they accept it. It is not a matter of the head but of the heart. They don't talk about God, they talk to God.

And for us from the modern world, the most misunderstood aspect of Eastern European village life is simply and without a doubt this religious world that the villagers live in. If we enter with them into their Church we will most likely be overwhelmed. It may strike us as exotic or even esoteric. It is vast paintings around the walls, clouds of incense and pictures that

Chapter Three: Discovering the Village World

are kissed. It is priests in resplendent vestments with embroidered clothes and golden vessels. It is a ritual chanted and sung without an instrument. It is people standing, kneeling, making prostrations and standing again. It is Orthodoxy.

The key to comprehending these rites is the awareness that they evolved in times when most people couldn't read or write. Their roots reach back to the days when the faith was proclaimed, taught, celebrated and passed on by means of ritual, art, drama, movement and music. This preliterate legacy from the first thousand years of Christianity is elaborately sensual. The incense is smelled, the pictures are seen, the chant is heard, the Holy Mysteries are tasted and the Holy Icon is touched with a kiss. Theology is sung. It is liturgical. It is painted, woven or embroidered. It is visual, sensual, and beautiful. When the procession circles the Church with banners waving and rich vestments glistening in the sun, one enters in, not with the intellect, but with one's feet, by walking, by joining the procession, by entering into the ritual.

Precisely because Eastern theology is so much acted out, painted, sung and sensual, it continues to stir the emotions, touch the psyche, reach the heart and nurture the soul in ways that tend to have atrophied in the rationalism of the West. Orthodoxy remains anchored in, and exposed to, the subconscious, the metaphysical or the spiritual realm. Here most marvelously,

the feminine remains close to the beating heart of the faith. The most common devotional focus of Eastern Orthodox Christianity is not the cross or a crucifix, but instead it is an icon of a Mother with a Child, most often in an embrace of affection. It is from this deep well of the soul, so far below the shallower waters of the mind, that our immigrant ancestors drank, and to this day the Old World continues to water its life.

    On the one hand, to discern the world of the village is to discover a life bound up with the earth. It is a life rooted in the traditions of the eternal struggle with nature. On the other hand, the villagers have found in their faith the triumph over this remorseless cycle of labor. Their faith gives meaning to their being. Farming is their way of life and faith is their way of understanding life. The two go inextricably together. The two form the traditional way of village life. The key to understanding the world of the village is to grasp the spiritual energy generated by a life lived so intimately with heaven and earth. The soul of the village is found in the vibrant spiritual dynamic between Creator, creature and creation. This traditional harmony between heaven, earth and humankind is the soil of the village soul, and it is in this soil that the roots of spirituality are so deeply sunk.

Chapter Four: We Build a Church

Chapter Four: We Build a Church

The building of the village Church was a most amazing adventure. It brought me the most majestic moments of my life, even though modesty suggests that I should hesitate to write about it.

In the summer of 1998, when I returned to Romania with a small group of pilgrims, I scheduled an afternoon visit to the village of the novice who had given me the vest. Alongside the beauty of the Romanian monasteries and churches, I wanted these pilgrims to also experience the marvelously rich interior of a peasant home. Arrangements were made, and on the appointed day we were welcomed into the home to admire the weaving and embroidery.

While we were there nibbling on the mounds of food that had been prepared for us, the mother of the family shyly informed us that this was a momentous day in their lives. Just that morning in the office of the mayor, the father of the family had signed the papers giving a portion of their land to the bishopric for the purpose of building a new Church. It was the portion of land that their son in the monastery would have inherited. The Church was to be for the one hundred or so families that now lived at this end of the village, some three to four kilometers distant from the large, new cement Church in the center of the village.

Our group was deeply touched by this act of generosity and we spontaneously collected a small gift

Chapter Four: We Build a Church

from among ourselves and presented it to the family. Then we all gathered outside on the newly donated field as the American Orthodox priest traveling with us blessed the land and set it aside for the building of the new Church.

Four months later, my wife and I returned to Romania for Christmas and we were amazed to discover that our small gift had made it possible to raise a beautifully carved cross on the road to mark the location of the new Church. It had also enabled the construction of a now nearly-finished outside altar. On Christmas day we attended the service in the great cement Church in the center of the village. We arrived early. The Church was without any heat. Inside it was around 25 degrees Fahrenheit (minus 5 Celsius). The cold crept up from the concrete, right into our bones. One could watch the breath of the priest emerge in clouds as he chanted the liturgy. By the middle of the service, when nearly 2,000 people crowded in and around the Church, my wife and I were so cold that my wife didn't want to stand back up after kneeling for the great entrance. She had decided that if she had to die sooner or later, freezing to death in a Church would be a rather blessed way to go. Later she was often to say that she had never been so spiritually warm and so physically cold. Our host sensed her pain and led her out of the Church. Later I found her in a cozy room cuddled up to a cookstove and warmed by liberal shots of schnapps.

That Christmas afternoon we were invited to visit the village priest. In the banter around the table of feast day delicacies, the topic of building the new Church finally came up. I expressed my desire that it be built out of wood. I had a particular fondness for the magnificent wooden architecture found all across the forests of Eastern Europe. Maramures had always built such majestic timber structures, until the modern passion for cement monstrosities eclipsed the tradition.

With dramatic gestures and a great flowing monologue that left our translator sputtering to keep up, the priest explained that a wooden Church was out of the question. Wood had simply become too expensive. He argued that we had to build with concrete. I protested. "How much would a wooden Church cost?" I asked him. "Too much," he replied, and so it went until at last in exasperation the priest asked to borrow my calculator. For a few minutes he sat at the table furiously punching numbers on the calculator. At last he sat back in his chair, cast us a somber look, and in a solemn voice he announced: "Mr. Currier. To build a Church out of wood would cost in your currency, in American dollars it would cost, fifteen-thousand dollars".

He repeated the words deliberately and precisely, as if in awe of the magnitude of the sum. My wife and I sat there for a moment, speechless. We were truly from two different worlds. Back home in the States we could barely consider building even a garage for $15,000, let alone a Church. Here $15,000 seemed an

Chapter Four: We Build a Church

unimaginable sum. That night after talking among ourselves, we decided that the cost of a wooden Church was a sum of money that we could entertain the task of raising. We asked God to help us do it.

During the summer of 1999, regular services were held in the field around the outside altar. It wasn't until June of the year 2000 that we were able to make our first offering. As I returned to the village, I carefully kept $5,000 wrapped in an envelope in a money belt. I told no one about it. As an honored guest I was invited to attend the celebration of the Divine Liturgy up inside the outside altar. At the end of the service I was asked to say a few words. I forgot everything I had rehearsed. I didn't know what to say or how to say it, so I stumbled along with some words about how I knew that they were all praying for their new Church and that my wife and I also desired to see the Church built. I mentioned something about God hearing their prayers and blessing them just as He had also heard our prayers and blessed us. So in a matter of seconds I arrived at the transitional: "therefore". I said: "Therefore God has made it possible for us to make, today, a contribution to the building of this Church in the sum of five-thousand United States dollars, or around one-hundred million Romanian lei." Florin, who was translating for me repeated the sum in dollars in a firm and clear voice, and then turned to me as the color drained out of his face. He looked at me for one of those seconds that seemed like an eternity, and a great "WHAT?" exploded from him. Embarrassed, I whispered in a soft voice: "One-hundred million Romanian lei!" He turned and thundered out across the valley: "One-hundred million lei"

Immediately, in a synchronized movement, every arm in the congregation rose to make the sign of the cross. People began to hug each other. Then some of the women fell down on their knees. People began to cry. I handed the envelope to the stunned priest and I began to cry. Now it seemed that everybody was crying.

Now as I tell this story, I have to write that in the slow motion of a split second, two insights struck me simultaneously. As the great tidal wave of emotional awe and thanksgiving rose up around me and roared toward me, I realized with brilliant clarity that God had used me. God had used us. Undeserving as we felt, God had used us to work the miracle that was the answer to the prayers of these people. It was too much for me. I was overwhelmed by the deluge of joy and gratitude that now crashed down around me. "No, no, no, not me," I whispered under my breath, " to God alone be the Glory."

In that same instant another insight dawned in my awareness, to grow more slowly as the day progressed. I knew with a blessed assurance that there wasn't another thing in the whole world that I could have spent that money on that could have given me anywhere near the satisfaction that this presentation had just unleashed. No car, boat, camera, toy or travel, could match the joy of giving this gift.

By mid afternoon of that June Sunday the whole village was awash in arguments as to how to begin to build the Church. Alas this is also the way of the village. It would be a wooden Church. That issue was settled in a flash. It would be dedicated to Saint Dimitru. The priest groaned under the challenge of organizing the permits and papers while the men of the congregation decided to dig the foundation. To this day I don't know if the architect drew the plans first and the foundation was dug according to them, or the men dug the foundation first and the architect fit the building on it.

Most Maramures men have building in their bones. They were born, so to speak, with an axe in their hands. Working with wood is certainly in their genes. The old Church down in the village dates from 1364. They don't really understand the architect, but they tolerate him. Whom they trust is the master builder and the skilled crew he assembles. So it was that stones were gathered, cement was purchased, the guidelines were staked out and on the appointed day in the late summer of the year 2000, sixty one men showed up with shovels and the priest with a bottle of schnapps and the foundation of the new Church went in.

Now the search for wood began. Word went out through the vines of family connections. Shepherds tending the flocks for the summer in the mountain meadows started inquiring among the forest workers.

On the 26th of October which is the feast day of St. Dumitru, the Bishop came to celebrate the Divine Liturgy for the festival. An altar room was built like a

Chapter Four: We Build a Church

stage on the new foundation and the congregation gathered around it.

Wood was finally located high on a mountainside along the Ukrainian border. A price was negotiated. The proper permits were granted by the forester, and that winter men from the village packed up their camping gear and trudged into the forest. For six weeks they camped out there, daily felling the trees from which their village Church would be built. Truckload by truckload the logs were hauled to the building site, laboriously squared off with a chainsaw and stacked to dry.

In that summer of 2000 all the master builders of the area were busy with other jobs so regular services were held in the field around the outdoor altar. The first wedding was preformed. The first graves were dug in the cemetery.

Among the many dreams for the new Church was, of course, the dream of having a bell. I had heard that some churches in Romania had received bells from Germany. The story was that during the Second World War the Nazi government of Germany had requisitioned all the church bells of the land and melted them down for making munitions. After the war many congregations had hastened to replace their bells but there was at that time neither the money nor the metal available to purchase quality bells. Now, some fifty years later, many well-off German congregations were removing these older postwar bells and replacing them with new quality castings. Thus these old bells were often available if you could find them.

A few inquires were made without results until I happened to run into a retired Roman Catholic priest in the market of a Black Forest town where we were visiting. I asked him if he knew of any bells. "Try Hoffstetten," he said, explaining that this little village Church had removed three bells and for a long time they had been trying to give them away. Straight away we drove out to Hoffstetten. The bells were there. They hung on the Church lawn in a tile-covered timber framework. Our hopes soared and then plummeted as we discovered a brass plaque announcing that the bells were now a memorial. They had been blessed and now hung in silence as an admonishment for all time that Church bells should never again be melted down for munitions. There was a pathos about the memorial. Could it be that the bells were pleading with us to rescue them?

Whatever the case, we were inspired. As eloquently as we could we penned our plea. We described the poor villagers building their own Church. We made their prayer for a Church bell palpable. We argued that bells were meant to ring. We imagined the Hofstetten bells resounding in the crisp air of the Carpathians. We portrayed their peal echoing up the mountainous valleys to summon the congregation to prayer. We pleaded for the gift of a bell, as an act of reconciliation, a gesture of love and a sign of peace.

Throughout the autumn of 2000 our request was debated, argued and discussed everywhere in Hofstetten. The Freiburg Diocesan office for Church Bells tested the bells and formally ruled that only the smaller of the three bells was in a condition to be considered for a gift. This helped. Finally, at the December meeting of the Hofstetten village counsel, a decision was reached. On Christmas day, a headline in the local newspaper announced the gift, trumpeting that now Christmas had truly come for this Orthodox congregation in Romania.

In the village of the Ieud, the jubilation was unbounded. It was another miracle. In the January snow the construction of the bell tower was begun. It was premature. There was still the problem of transporting a thousand- pound bell a thousand miles across four borders. Months passed. The proper papers were organized and authorized. An American tourist group donated the needed funds and finally a Hungarian trucker was found to transport the load. In early July of 2001, a forklift in Germany hoisted the bell on to the truck and it headed for Romania.

The next episode was the drama of the delivery. The Hungarian truck driver didn't speak a word of Romanian. He told the story as follows. From Budapest he telephoned the village to announce his arrival the following day. The village priest arranged to meet him at the border to avoid any attempts at bribery. The priest waited all day at the border before he finally gave up and returned home. There the priest found the Hungarian truck with the bell parked in front of his house. Somehow without speaking a word of Romanian, the trucker had miraculously managed to get the bell through Romanian customs and find his way to the village. It was too late to unload the bell in the dark, so the priest invited the trucker to spend the night, and the two of them sat down to a bountiful supper. At seven the next morning, the heavy truck crawled along the dirt road up the valley to the site of the Church, turned into the yard and promptly sank up to the axel in the soft earth. In the words of the trucker, he was terrified. He couldn't speak the language, he was alone with a priest in a field with a thousand-pound bell to unload, and his truck was mired. Then a most amazing thing happened. From everywhere men began to appear. They called to others working in neighboring fields. They grabbed timbers and wedged them under the bell and gracefully lifted it off the truck. Then they gathered around the truck, and lifted it out of the mud and helped it back onto the road. "I have never experienced anything like it," the driver confessed when he returned to Germany with his next load.

Within weeks, a yoke had been crafted for the bell and was hung in its new tower. Following the Divine Liturgy on Sunday August 12th, the priests led the congregation from the outside altar to the bell tower and solemnly blessed the new bell. There it was reborn to its new life of daily calling the faithful to prayer. There was weeping in the valley.

Chapter Four: We Build a Church

So grateful were the villagers that they commissioned an icon of the Mother of God from the Monastery of Rohia. In December, the priest and two young men traveled by train from Romania to Hofstetten in Germany. There, the young men dressed in their colorful traditional costumes attended the Sunday Roman Catholic Mass and presented the Hofstetten congregation with the icon as a gesture of gratitude and thanksgiving. Young Germans in traditional dress received the gift. Now the Germans wept.

By midsummer of 2001, the village master builders were free to direct the construction of the Church. Volunteers from the congregation joined the crew. Every morning they would arrive, often before the sun was over the hills. One by one the logs were taken from the stack, carefully notched and painstakingly fitted onto the foundation. Slowly, day by day and log by log throughout the long summer days, the building began to rise. Women took turns bringing the noon lunch. Every evening as the shadows lengthened and the men needed to return home for their chores, the master would call an end to the labor and all the workers would form a circle to pray before passing around the bottle for a parting drink.

Prayer and schnapps are par for the course of the village. Also a little intrigue around the edges is to be anticipated. One day in the village, two truck loads of logs from the forest appeared to be missing. It seemed that someone had stolen them. After all, when one has camped out in the snow to cut the timber, one is well aware of the amount of logs that should have been delivered to the building site, especially for a Church. Insinuations soon brewed into a storm. As time and transportation permitted, the trail was followed back up into the forest and out again. The evidence was quite conclusive, but confronting the culprit elicited only outrage. It was someone who had given endless hours of labor to the building. In village logic, wasn't someone who milked the cow allowed to spoon off a couple licks of cream? The records were hopeless. They were scrupulously kept, in pencil. I often wondered which end of the pencil wore away the fastest. For a while tempers raged, tongues wagged, and some peo-

Chapter Four: We Build a Church

ple were seriously offended. No confession was ever made but with time forgiveness was asked and with prayers and schnapps the wounds ceased to itch and life went on.

By September the walls were up and the steeple began to rise inside a towering wooden scaffold. The crew turned to shaving shingles. With an axe, they skillfully split two foot long logs into rough shingle-length boards. Then, sitting on special saw horses, they clamped the boards in front of them by putting pressure on a hinged hook with their feet and individually shaped each shingle with a draw blade. Buckets of shingles were swept aloft on a rope to the workers at the top of the steeple. Before the Church was finished, its roofs would be covered by over 180,000 shingles.

Late on the afternoon of October 20th, 2001, a horse-drawn wagon rattled into the yard carrying the eight foot tall sheet metal cross for the top of the tower. It had been made by the Gypsies who are the tinsmiths, or the tinkers, of all of Eastern Europe. Early on Monday morning October 27th, the two priests from down in the village gathered with the congregation before the cross in front of the Church. Even the children were there. On a day such as this, the start of school could wait. Solemnly the priest blessed the cross. Then, starting with the master builder, the men lined up and, crossing themselves, one by one they kissed the cross. The men were followed by the women and all the children. Finally a rope was tied around this crown for the Church, and as four men put their shoulders to a make-

shift windlass, it lifted off the ground. Old Gavril put his whole soul into ringing the bell and its peals thundered down the valley. Eyes filled with tears and people cried openly as the great cross, glistening in the sun, moved slowly upwards along the scaffolding. Finally four men at the top wrestled it over the rim of the scaffold and nailed it securely to the top of the steeple, over 100 feet above the valley.

Construction stopped for the winter, but by February of 2002 the crew reappeared, the rounded arches for the ceiling were raised and the steep pointed arches for the roof were secured above them. Day by day the building took form. Slowly the roof went up. and the scaffold came down. By June the basic structure was finished. The Bishop ordained a young priest and sent him and his wife to serve in the new Church.

Through generous gifts from many friends we were able to pay off our pledge and add a little more. Significant contributions came from many corners. Villagers working abroad were solicited for donations. The congregation gave sacrificially. The money poured in. Still new needs were announced almost weekly.

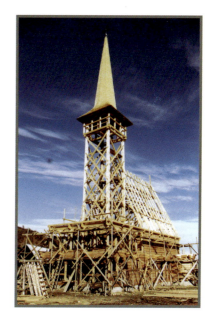

Chapter Four: We Build a Church

Who knows how much the bucket leaked? An old saying in Orthodoxy claims that when the faithful build a Church, the Devil builds a Chapel nearby. Simple figures suggested that the Devil was acquiring a rather substantial structure. Tempers flared again but soon cooled down. Just as the new world takes construction cost overruns for granted, the old world understands that the Devil will always use the temptation of a pot of money to seduce a few weak souls. Why even fret about it? It is obvious who won. The majestic Church stands gleaming in the sun. As the final touches were put on the building, contributions trailed off, the final bills were paid and nothing was left. The total cost had come to around $26,000 U.S. dollars.

Now the women of the congregation went to work. Over a weekend they gathered special plants in the forest. The following Monday they assembled at the Church to cook up a dye by boiling down the plants. All day they took turns tending the fires under the cooking kettles of dye. On Tuesday morning they brought bundles of wool, and again for a whole day they tended the fires as they dyed the wool. One lady took over the task of weaving, and when I returned to the village a month later, a forty foot long carpet led from the front door to the altar of the Church.

A woodcutter in the next village was commissioned to carve the structure for the iconostasis, and over the winter of 2002-2003 the elaborately carved structure appeared piece after piece out of the clutter and shavings of his workroom. In Iasi a group of devout young painters were given the com-

Shadows of Yesterday

mission for the icons and even as I write in this summer of 2004 they are finishing their work. The Church now finally is approaching that glorious day of its consecration. And that's where the story ends, for now.

Chapter Five: To Life, Raw and Tender

53

Chapter Five: To Life, Raw and Tender

For the most part village life is pretty rough, rugged and raw. Nothing is very subtle. They accomplish most of their tasks by muscle and strength; banging, hammering or chopping their way along. If they need to build a Church tower one hundred feet high, they simply nail up a scaffold to build from. If they need power to run a mill, they damnup a river and build a sluice for the water to drive the massive hand hewn gears that turn their mill stone. Only in one area have I sensed a sort of restrained concentration that approaches daintiness. This is reflected in the finesse with which they attend to the process of distillation.

Distillation is a delicate process. Somewhere back in the mists of time, human beings discovered that almost any rotting grain or fruit produces a substance that we have come to know as alcohol. They also discovered that this alcohol has an interesting effect on the human mood. People like it. However, the challenge was to separate or extract the alcohol out of the unappealing mash of rotten grain or fruit. A breakthrough came when someone discovered that when the mash of rotten grain or fruit is cooked, the alcohol in the mash turns into steam just a hair before the rest of the liquid in the mash. This fact presented the great challenge of developing a way to turn the alcohol in the mash into steam just before the other juices of the mash turned into steam, and then to cool

Chapter Five: To Life, Raw and Tender

and condense that alcoholic steam down fast enough to separate the alcohol out of the rotten mash. This process demands unaccustomed delicacy and villgers achieve it by tending an elaborate contraption which is known as a still.

The alcoholic product thus distilled goes by various names. In English it is generally known as distilled spirits or simply spirits, but I prefer to use the German or Dutch term, which is schnapps. Because there is always a little bit of steam from the rest of the mash that condenses along with the alcohol, most schnapps will have a little taste of whatever grain or fruit it came from. Schnapps is always a clear liquid. At best it can be around eighty percent pure alcohol, and of course, drinking eighty percent pure alcohol can be lethal. Therefore the schnapps fresh from the still is usually diluted with either water or fruit juice.

Schnapps with an alcohol content of fifty percent is called 100 proof. Most schnapps for sale in the USA is not more than 38% alcohol but schnapps in the village can run as high as 65% alcohol, or nearly 130 proof. In Russia and Poland, the common schnapps made from potatoes or rye is known as Vodka. In the Balkans it is called Slivovitz or Rakija, and in Romania it is most often made from plums and known as Tuica. If it is put through the distillation process twice, it is called Palinka, or Horinka.

Whatever it is called, it is everywhere. It is more than just booze. It serves a strange sort of surrogate sacramental function. It is the raw reflection of the Holy Mysteries in the Church. It flows at every occasion. It is the obligatory welcome and departure drink, the mandatory seal of every deal and the compulsory rite for honoring both the living and the dead.

Years ago, on one of my first visits to Romania I was maneuvering my way along a snowy village road when I glimpsed a colorfully decorated horse through an open gate. I carefully stopped the car and backed up. A few men stood in

Chapter Five: To Life, Raw and Tender

and most of the young people were in traditional dress. We had the only cameras to record the occasion so individuals and groupings requested pictures and lined up to pose for us. Cautiously, our interpreter informed us that our arrival had interrupted the traditional wedding preparations of the bride. Quietly, he encouraged us to melt back into the space that had been cleared for us in the crowded room. It was time for the bride to prepare to leave her parental home. In both the home of the bride and the groom, this leave taking is a ritual that is an essential and traditional part of the wedding.

The seventeen-year-old bride took her place behind the table in the corner under the icon. A single glass bottle of Tuica was set before her along with a few small shot glasses. The room grew silent

the yard. I knew just enough Romanian to greet them with the customary, "Doamne Ajuta" or "God preserve us", and gesturing at my camera, I asked if I might photograph the horse. I was enthusiastically welcomed and a handful of men immediately rushed across the road to invite my companions to pile out of the car. It turned out that the horse was garlanded to accompany the bride to the Church for her wedding. We had arrived at the bride's house and now we were invited to the wedding. We entered the single large room of the house. It was beautifully hung with embroidered towels

as the bride's father approached the table. Two glasses were filled. Father and daughter gazed into each other's eyes and raising the glasses, the father spoke something like this. "My darling, I have loved you with my whole heart. As God is my witness, I have tried my best to be a good, kind and loving father. In all that I have failed to be what I wanted to be, I ask you to forgive me. Now as you go forth from my house, I give you my blessing. I pray you will be a credit to this home and a blessing in your new home."

By this time great tears were rolling down the cheeks of the young girl. Yet she held her glass high and steady, as she looked into her father's eyes. "I thank God," she started haltingly, "for everything that you have given me. I love you and I pray to God that I will be a credit to this house and in my husband's home. Please forgive me everything that I have done that has hurt you. I love you. Good bye." Slowly the two glasses moved toward each other, clinked, and returned to their respective lips. The father drained his glass in one gulp but the bride only sipped hers as she had many farewells to make on this afternoon. Next her mother came forward, and tears so overwhelmed the mother and daughter that all their words were lost and only a soft "tink" of the two glasses sealed their parting. After the father and mother there came brothers, sisters, grandparents, aunts and uncles until the bottle was nearly empty.

I stood silently and watched. Life in the village is raw. The pain of the parting is pure. So is the Tuica. It is always 100 proof if not stronger. It burns going down, and yet I had just seen it used so tenderly.

Chapter Five: To Life, Raw and Tender

Soon thereafter I was allowed to witness another fascinating ritual, even though only women were supposed to be present. It is called the "signing" or "the giving of the sign." It takes place on the day of the formal engagement. In the old days most marriages were arranged. The Godparents of the groom would bargain with the bride's father until a wedding was agreed upon. The contract for the marriage would be made by the men of the respective families. In marriage the bride would leave the home of her parents to become a part of the family of her husband. It is not too harsh to say that essentially the bride was sold to the groom and his family. However, even today when couples more often find each other, the engagement is never certain, until a sign is given that the women also agree. It was to this traditional giving of the sign that I was invited.

In the afternoon of the day of the formal engagement, the mother of the groom and matriarch of the family sets off with an entourage of five to seven other women of her family to visit the bride-to-be. Solemnly she enters the home of the girl and stands before her. Placing her hand under her heavy woolen apron she offers her hand to the young woman. The bride-to-be in turn places her hand under her woolen apron. The aprons must be woolen because wool symbolizes prosperity. Privately, almost secretly, the two women shake hands under their respective aprons.

In this gesture the mother-in-law accepts the new bride into her household and the bride-to-be submits to her mother-in-law. But that is only half of the sign. The bride-to-be responds to the secret handshake by pouring two shots of Tuica and offering one to the groom's mother. This toast is the public signal that the two women have agreed and the engagement is now officially on. Everyone joins in celebrating. Tuica both seals the engagement and fuels the celebration of it.

Later the groom arrives and takes his fiancé to the Church where the priest blesses the engagement. In the evening, it is obligatory that each of the groom's friends bring a bottle to the bride's home to celebrate and seal the engagement. As in life, so it is in death. When a funeral ends and the tight mass of mourners starts to loosen, women with large woven sacks hurry ahead to the cemetery gate. Out of their sacks they pull freshly fried, sugar covered pastries. Not to accept one is to offend the departed, for only as the mourners are strengthened by eating, do they join in strengthening the departed for his or her journey. Likewise, as the sugar coated pastries sweeten the way home for the mourners, so is the way of the departed sweetened. Men appear immediately beside the women, planting themselves in the center of the path with bottle and glasses in hand. Sharing a goodbye shot with the deceased is a social obligation.

Chapter Five: To Life, Raw and Tender

Similarly, at the memorial services on the anniversary of a death or at the annual All Saints Day service in the cemetery, a drink with the departed is obligatory.

Of course there is alcoholism in the village. There is abuse, violence and despair. No one denies this. In a village, everyone knows everything about everybody. As best they can, women surround and take care of suffering wives. Men surround, isolate, and sometimes even mete out a crude sort of justice to abusive husbands. Life in the village is raw. It is a cross we bear. Tuica is a medicine for its pain and it causes pain. Like the cross itself, it is ambiguous; it brings death and life. It both blesses and curses. It is a cursed blessing and a blessed curse, and thank God there is always a shoulder to lean on when the legs are too wobbly for walking. It's all part of life.

Shadows of Yesterday

Shadows of Yesterday

Chapter Six: Mountains, Markets, and Memorial Towels

The first Sunday of May is milking day. It reflects the deep bond of the peasant with nature. All across the mountainous backbone of Europe, the poor peasant farmers who keep animals are obliged by the nature of the landscape to move their herds to the high mountain pastures for the summer. The small farms in the valleys where they live, barely yield enough food for survival. Every inch of land is used for the house, sheds, gardens, orchards, and field crops. There is no land left over for grazing. But as the snow melts from the mountains above, lush meadows appear on the high distant slopes. It is then the time for milking day.

On milking day the sheep that will spend the summer on the mountains are assembled and milked. Each man measures just how much milk is given and according to this measure his portion of the summer cheese is reckoned. Usually, related families will assemble their cows, horses and flocks of sheep into a single herd. When all is ready, the priest comes to bless the herd and herdsmen, and they make their way down the road, out of the village and off into the mountains. Sometimes they travel for days.

For the long months of the summer, the animals remain off in the mountains. They are tended by young boys from the village that are under the charge of an older man who is experienced in tending the herds and

Shadows of Yesterday

making cheese. Three times a day the sheep are milked. Everyday the milk is cooked, hung in cloths to drain, and made into cheese. Once a week, a horse and wagon sets out from the village to bring supplies to the summer camp and to collect the cheese. I have joined in such a journey.

As the road turns from asphalt to gravel, and from gravel to earth, and from an earthen lane to a rugged trail over rocks and roots, a portentous feeling is awakened. The forest feels alive. The horse strains and the wagon groans. The trees thicken into darkness. I could easily be afraid up here. Then a glade appears. Then another and another. The dark thickness of the forest gives way. Slowly the glades grow larger and the trees grow thinner. The way levels, and we emerge on the rolling green of the mountaintop. Visible is a large wooden cross, a corral for the animals and the lean-to where the cheese is cooked and the man and boys sleep.

On the day that I am describing, light rains kept sweeping across the mountain meadow. We arrived around noon just as the boys were coming in out of the mists with their clusters of animals for the mid-day milking. I watched them with wonderment. They strode along like grown men in boys' bodies. Each was in his early- to mid-teens. Each had his own personality but each also shyly or innocently radiated a kind of mature confidence. They had learned the complex wiles and ways of nature and knew how to face the wolves and bears that regularly raided the herd. They had such

Chapter Six: Mountains, Markets, and Memorial Towels

a gentle rapport with their animals. They had poise. I envied them the education of this experience. They were at home with being alone in the forest, with being alone with their animals and with being alone with themselves.

We shared a mountain meal of Tuica and "balmos," a rich mixture of butter, cheese and sour cream cooked into corn meal mush. The boys wandered off again with their animals. The sky cleared as the afternoon wore on and distant vistas appeared. The ridge lines faded off into infinity in ever lightening shades. A mountain meadow is an awesome place. It has a spiritual feel about it. In the thick silence even the softest of sounds seem to echo forever. As we loaded the cheese, said goodbye and rattled off, I wondered what it would be like to be up here for a summer as a boy. What kind of a man would it make? In pondering the answers to these questions, I felt I was beginning to understand what forces formed our immigrant ancestors. I felt I was beginning to grasp where they came from.

As the wagon rolled into the village, it began to stop and deliver heads of cheese at various houses. Here a head was left in payment for this and there another was left in payment for something else. It is not completely fair to say that there is no money in the village. Money has been around for a long time. It is always needed for things like taxes, fees, dues and levies. What is fair to say, is that the economy of the village operates essentially through trading and barter.

Shadows of Yesterday

town. Crowds mill through the animals being offered. They visit, gossip, tease, laugh and barter. They drink. Piglets squeal, chickens squawk and sheep bleat. A piglet is often put in a sack to be carried home, and the saying, "Don't buy a pig in a poke," comes from the sly trick of putting a cat in the bag instead of a piglet. The reference to "not letting the cat out of the bag," also comes from this deception.

Craftsmen and vendors set up their stands just beyond the animals. The craftsmen offer things like shoes, belts and work tools made out of wood. The vendors offer a variety of everything from hats to hardware, from yard goods to sewing supplies. Food stands feed the milling crowds.

Nowhere is this more obvious than at the regularly held markets. In an established monthly order, market days move from town to town, up and down the valley. This allows the itinerant vendors to move with them and cover the territory. In all the towns around, everyone knows when and where the markets are.

Markets are a marvelous kaleidoscope of life. On market day chores are moved up to before daw, and by sunrise the roads are full of people walking, people leading animals horse-drawn wagons loaded with people and horse drawn wagons loaded with people and animals, all heading to the market

Chapter Six: Mountains, Markets, and Memorial Towels

I am always amazed at the villagers' mastery of the intricate complexity of relationships, traditions and customs. Not only does everybody seem to know each other but they also recognize each other's animals. I have often heard someone at a market protest: "but I know he's here, I saw his horse over there!" Or there are the dictates of tradition. We learned the hard way that only fabric with a pattern of little flowers may be used for girls' skirts. A mother once asked us if we could bring some material for her to sew skirts for her daughters. In all innocence my wife bought some lovely cloth with a colorful paisley pattern. We were both perplexed when something akin to a look of horror crossed the face of the mother when she accepted our gift. We learned later that it was just

understood that virginity is a flower and that little girls wear flowers. The look of horror on the mother's face was simply her perplexity in trying to imagine what message her daughters would be sending out if they sashayed down the lane in paisley skirts.

The web of control woven by customs and rules can be oppressive and stifling. A few years ago I received the great tribute of being made an honorary citizen of the village. The mayor presented a plaque, the priest

Shadows of Yesterday

prayed and the little girls in traditional dress lined up to give me bouquets of flowers. A few days later I went out to the woodshed to get some fuel for the fire, and pandemonium broke out. The girls, boys and mother, in fact everyone in sight, came running to carry the wood for me. I was accepted all right, but I was accepted at the rank of patron. I was accepted but I was scolded. What would the neighbors think if they saw that I was left to carry my own firewood? So being accepted demanded that I accept the fact that I had to be waited on. Thank God I have been given a sense of humor. I was really a part of the farm. If I ever entertained any illusions of grandeur, my position on the feeding roster placed my pretensions in perspective. Every morning the family rose and dutifully fed the chickens, the cow, the horse, the pig and the patron.

For the most part, the web of the village world is invisible. Like the lessons learned by a boy tending sheep on the mountain, or the flowers on a little girl's skirt or the rules of rank, the ways of the village are just there. They are unconscious. They are assumed. They are taken for granted. But every now and then someone will come, stop, look and ask a question. What is this? Why do you do that? And in the answer to these questions a new layer of village life is unveiled. Astonishing discoveries are made. Treasures are found.

One such phenomenon is that of the towels. Homes and churches are full of them, and yet they often

go unnoticed. They sort of get lost amid the color of a cottage or the busyness of a Church. However, once they are noticed, their ubiquity is amazing. They are draped around the icons and given to mourners at funerals. In the North, they are worn at weddings, and in death they are tied to the cross in the cemetery. They are woven in almost every home. Every household has them. Wardrobes are filled with them. Churches are sometimes hung so thick with towels that they almost hide the iconostasis. When the families wash them before some great feast, in village after village whole clotheslines are festooned with them.

These towels are found all across Orthodox Eastern Europe, from Karelia on the White Sea to the

Chapter Six: Mountains, Markets, and Memorial Towels

Mediterranean shores of the Balkans. Each culture and language has its own special name for them. They are a most fascinating phenomenon. On the one hand they are amazingly similar, generally running about two yards long and around a foot wide, most often made of linen and decorated at both ends. Yet ,on the other hand, they vary dramatically in decorative designs, patterns, motifs and colors.

On the surface they are simply functional. They are for washing, wiping and drying. It is the many other and varied ways that they are used, and their elaborate decoration, that hints at the deeper roots of their meaning and origin. Thanks to the seminal research of Dr. Mary Kelly, we now know that many of the recurring symbols and motifs of these towels can be traced back to pre-Christian feminine and fertility rituals. Their origin is in ancient rituals and rites of protection and empowerment. To this day, millennia later, they still carry overtones of these ritual powers. They are not for sale. They are created to be given away. This fact alone clearly signals that they belong to a world of values different from our modern ways. They are uniquely a part of the women's world. They are made by women. The traditional style of each area is passed on from mother to daughter. This hints that they carry with them something deeply personal that is beyond being given a price. They carry some power of the person who wove them. They carry some

Shadows of Yesterday

mysterious energy of the soul. They are coin of a different realm. I call them a currency of love. Their exchange among the villagers is beyond the understanding of rationality. They approach something of the mystical.

Unfortunately, today the modern world is rapidly eroding these older feelings and inherited understandings. Everywhere the towels are still being woven, but the arrival of market day vendors offering embroidery and weaving yarns in vivid colors has fostered a new fashion. Towels are now appearing decorated in electric colors, with quivering pinks and vibrating magentas. Although in some back valleys, millennia-old pre-Christian motifs still appear with amazing regularity, reproductions of sentimental religious calendar art has also increasingly come into vogue.

It is at a funeral that the ritual role of the towels emerges most obviously. Years ago, I happened to be walking with a village friend when he casually commented that his mother had woven around 300 towels for her funeral. I stopped and looked at him in astonishment.

Chapter Six: Mountains, Markets, and Memorial Towels

"What for," I asked. "Pomana," he answered simply, and so began my initiation into yet another dimension of the village experience.

"Pomana" is a Slavic word that basically means "memorial.". I began to grasp the role of these towels on the day that I accompanied the nuns of Dobric monastery to the funeral of a young woman in the neighboring village. The body had been laid out in the fine room of the farm house. Now a space had been cleared out and cleaned up in one of the sheds in the yard. It had been hung with woven rugs. The open coffin was carried out and placed on two saw horses in the shed. The yard was filled with mourners. On one side a phalanx of old women wrapped in black, lined a bench. Others stood behind them. Grim, weathered faces peered out from under black scarves. Gnarled hands rested on black aprons. Men stood around the edges, their coats hung over their shoulders in the heat. From the house, women carried the belongings of the deceased woman out to the shed, and her husband, choking on his sobs, passed them over her open coffin into the hands of a little woman who would give them to the poor of the village.

Following the final prayers, amid wrenching cries, the cover was tightened onto the coffin, and the coffin was placed on a wagon. Slowly the procession made its way through the village, stopping in front of

Shadows of Yesterday

the homes of relatives to read the Gospels and offer prayers. In the cemetery, an icon wrapped in a beautiful towel rested at the bottom of the grave. With the pronouncement of the final benediction, a cacophony of wailing and lamentation rose up as the coffin was slowly lowered into the grave. Now the women who had accompanied the cortege to the burial gave elaborately decorated towels to the priest, the pall bearers, the banner carriers, the crucifer and a few other special mourners.

As the mourners headed back to the memorial

Chapter Six: Mountains, Markets, and Memorial Towels

meal, women handed out fried breads and men poured Tuica at the cemetery gate. Back at the house during the meal, as the priest blessed the home following this visitation of death, still more towels appeared. Everyone present received one.

It was quite sometime later before the full impact of what I had experienced was brought home to me. In the meantime, I had inquired about towels, and in a number of homes older women had shown me the large collections that they had woven for their funerals. Then one day, the young nun at the monastery where I was staying got called home by the death of her grandmother. When she returned a few days later, she showed me the "Pomana" her grandmother had woven. It was a simple hand towel. Sister Violetta gently folded the towel around her hands and wiped her face where tears were forming. As she did this, she smiled at me with her glistening eyes and said very softly, "every time I dry my face with this, it will be like my Granny comforting me, wiping away my tears, and saying: 'It's all right my little Violet, God will take care of us."

Chapter Seven: The Wedding

75

Chapter Seven: The Wedding

A few years ago a glitzy travel magazine printed an article about the new upscale accommodations of Poland. In the middle of the article, the author went on in detail about becoming stuck behind a wedding procession on a country road. He fumed about the musicians, the wedding party and the frolicking guests that obstructed his way for a couple of miles. The two miles stretched into a whole paragraph. After he finally passed the procession and reached his destination, he celebrated his arrival by writing how good it felt to return to civilization. Now I fumed! I found his snobbery provocative. Then slowly my fuming simmered down to pity. What a chance he missed! Why didn't he plant his car beside the road and let himself go for once? Poor fool. Nothing beats a Polish wedding. Not only would he have been welcome, but he would have rivaled the bride and groom as the center of attention. As Grandma would have said: "Heda hada ball!"

A wedding is about bedding. Everyone in the village is aware of that. They know about reproduction. They are farmers. They keep animals. They understand that mating is essential to survival. On this point they comprehend clearly their kinship with their cattle. They appreciate the intensity of the drive to mate, as well as the delight of its pleasure. Yet precisely because they are so intimate with this reproductive energy, they also

Chapter Seven: The Wedding

grasp the chaos that it can create if it is uncontrolled. Boars and bucks need timber fences. Bulls need a ring in their nose, and village boys and girls need stern absolute rules. Strict and severe social control of sexual intimacy is an essential and accepted fact of life in the village. Mating is never just a matter between two people. Therefore the whole village sanctions, sanctifies and celebrates it with a wedding.

Village culture is patriarchal. The bride moves into the family of the groom. Everyone in a boy's family takes an interest in whomever the son of the family is eyeing. The girl's family also watches who is eyeing their daughter. Family status and station are at stake. Family rank, wealth and holdings are involved. A couple may have known each other since childhood or they may have met by chance, working in the fields or while attending a feast day or a funeral. Yet no matter how privately the chemistry of courtship is conjured up, the courtship itself takes place in the open. According to tradition, it is played out on the village stage. On Sunday afternoon the young men and women promenade in public in the center of the village. In former times they also joined in traditional dances. In some villages they still do. Everyone watches this ritual. Every nuance of contact is weighed and considered.

The Sunday posturing in the center of the village is disquietingly similar to the cattle market on Monday morning. Any prospective bride is carefully scrutinized. Will she be a good worker? Can she last the day in the field like a man and birth a baby every year? Is she a trouble maker and a gossip? What about her family? Are they no-goods? Lazy? Drunkards? What kind of a dowry will she bring? Will being bonded with her family be an asset or a liability? What will she inherit? So it goes, on and on. Life is raw in the village. The quality of breeding stock is as important for the marriage bed as it is for the barn.

I have seen one young bride pressured into a union that she felt much less than eager about. My heart went out to her, although I had a suspicion that the gangly awkward young man who so joyously received her might just turn out to be a most gentle, devoted and loving husband. On the less serious side I have seen parents agonize over their son's attraction to a city girl "with polish on her nails and no calluses on her hands." Yet for the most part weddings are tumultuously joyous affairs. My words and pictures can only hint at the layers of customs and celebrations that unfold throughout this event. Except, perhaps, for some religious rites, nothing equals the richness, vitality and exuberance of a traditional village wedding.

Once a marriage has been agreed upon and the engagement blessed by the priest, the count-down to the wedding begins. Normally it lasts just over the three Sundays that it takes for the "banns," or the intention to marry, to be announced in the Church. This public announcement invites any who might have any objection to the marriage to now make it known or forever after to hold their peace. This invitation is interesting. It is a ritualized wiping clean of the record. It warns any who might have some simmering suspicions or anger that now is their time to speak. It is now or never. With this rite, the village presents the couple a clean slate for the beginning of their new life.

Next, the negotiations begin for the music and the food. The priest may marry the couple, but it is the musicians who will accompany them non-stop through the nearly twenty four hours of ritual and celebration. Music starts in the morning. The Church service is usually around sunset, and the feast lasts all night. The musicians must fiddle for the dance of the groom's flag, the dance of the bride's crown, the dance of the hen and all the customary songs of the age-old repertoire for a wedding. All across Eastern Europe one

Chapter Seven: The Wedding

finds similar selections of wedding music. They probably all trace their roots to the wandering Gypsy musicians. Gypsies are famous for their music. It is one of the few occupations allowed them by the deep-set prejudices of the community. For their wedding, a couple will often favor the Gypsies who live around the fringe of their village. Gypsies may exist in abject poverty but when they touch their bow to the strings of their instrument, they soar majestically and everyone around looks up to them in admiration and awe.

Villagers also play. The traditional combination of a fiddle, guitar and drum, often enlivens long evenings as well as parties and celebrations. I was once deeply moved to meet a boy of thirteen who had found an old fiddle on his farm. With painstaking love he patched it up and taught himself to play. Some friends donated money to buy him a better and newer violin, and by the age of fifteen he had mastered an astonishing repertoire of village music. I could hardly believe that I had actually met a living link to this extraordinary world of ancient folk music.

Shadows of Yesterday

As for the wedding food, there are women in most villages who hire themselves out to organize the feasting. In some places there are women who volunteer just for the sheer love of being in control and creating massive meals. With the help of family and village friends the days before the wedding will be filled with circles of women filling massive kettles with cabbage rolls, preparing meats and baking sweets.

The couple themselves take on the task of inviting the guests, wandering the village lanes in their festive finery with their wedding candles and a bottle of Tuica to invite their relatives and friends to their wedding.

Chapter Seven: The Wedding

As the day of the wedding draws closer, the excitement surrounding the preparation of the bride and the groom increases. In the teasing and innuendos of the male friends of the groom, there is a clear awareness that they are losing their buddy from their circle of bachelor freedom, frolicking and carousing. This loss saddens them. On the other hand their buddy will now be entering into the pleasurable enjoyment of marital intimacy. This they celebrate. Together they gather at the groom's house to "sew" his flag. Black, white, green, and red colored scarves and embroidered handkerchiefs donated by female friends are bound to a long stout pole. Black for it is the color of the groom's hat and links him with the dead who have gone before. White, for it is the color of the brides crown and announces her virginity. Green, for it symbolizes the freshness of nature, growth, and fertility; and red, because it is the color of burning love. Individuals may adorn the pole with private totems such as ribbons or jewelry. Only red thread is used to sew or bind the flag to its pole, for it is inflamed love that binds the marriage together. A mirror may be attached to ward off evil spirits. Fresh greenery crowns the pole.

The best man bears the flag throughout the wedding. As the time approaches for the groom to leave his home the best man gathers all the groom's friends and buddies, and holding high the decorated pole, he leads them into the dance of the groom's flag. Older males may join the circle but never a woman. With small steps, he moves clockwise around the groom to music similar to that played for the Sunday dances in the village square. This dance marks the

Shadows of Yesterday

separation of the groom from the joys of youth, courtship and bachelorhood. It underscores the end of a phase of the life cycle. As the pulse of the music and dance throbs through the room the dancers shout improvised or traditional rhymed proverbs.

"No more sweet hearts in your life!
Now only one, and she's your wife!"
"Choose well a lass who does nothing lack,
For from this deal, you can't turn back!"

The flag swirls, the fiddle sings and the drum beats to stomping feet. The dance goes on and on. The shouts grow ribald. When the dancers and musicians have exhausted themselves, the flag bearer signals the end of the dance by slowly circling the flag three times horizontally over the heads of the circle while reciting:

"When the year has covered its span,
there should be born your little Dan,
and by the end of the second year,
a little Mike or Nick, so dear!"

The dance of the flag is followed by the leave-taking ceremony of the groom and the departure for the Church. With his best man carrying his flag that proclaims his masculinity, strength and virility, the groom goes forth to crown his life by taking a wife. His buddies follow him toward his fulfillment calling him "our King" or "our Prince".

The so called "dressing of the bride" is a lot more somber. The center of the ceremony is the

Chapter Seven: The Wedding

braiding of the bride's hair. Once she is privately dressed in her white wedding clothes, she is seated in the center of the room. Older women comb her hair and begin to braid it, working in strands of fresh greenery for fertility and binding them with the white ribbons given her by her husband-to-be as his claim on her purity. As the hair is lovingly combed and braided, the musicians take up the solemn melodies of the occasion. It is time for the lamenting. Slowly it builds. In waves it comes. The young girls lament the departure of the bride from their circle. They shout their rhymed couplets out onto the musician's chords. The lament swells to encompass the departure of the bride from her family home, her mother, her sisters, her aunts. Older women cry with the memories of their own separations. The miseries of marriage are given full vent. The bride cries. She is expected to cry. If the occasion itself isn't enough, onions are enlisted to assist her.

Once her hair is braided the bridesmaid who is the maid of honor, takes up the bride's crown and, holding it aloft, she chooses a male partner and moves out into the dance of the bride's crown. The music modulates into a tune that couples dance to. Couples join in the circle, following the crown as they dance around the bride. The symbolism is transparent. The bride's crown is her maidenhood being offered up to her husband.

As the dance ends, the crown is placed on the bride's head, and quite quietly a large white scarf

appears. It is often silk or satin. The bridesmaid gives one end to the bride and she holds the other end. The symbolism is anything but subtle. On this silken scarf the marriage will be consummated. Now through the hours of ceremony, it will bind for the last time the bride-to-be, through her maid of honor, to her maidenhood. With the scarf in hand, the leave-taking begins. With the last toasts and tears of this ritual, the parties of the bride and the groom leave their respective homes for the Church. If possible they will walk the whole way but if the way is longer they will travel with horse and wagon, dismounting only to walk through the village center to the Church. The way to the Church is one of the high points of the wedding. Everyone turns out to watch the parade. Down the lane lined with well wishers, the bride and groom make their way as royalty, each with their own musicians and festive costumed entourage.

At the Church, only the immediate party enters. Traditionally the groom's party arrives first and waits for the bride to arrive. Custom allows the bride to take her time, for this walk to the altar will be the last chance of her lifetime for her to set her own pace. The old women warn her not to be too slow. Entering the Church, the bride takes her place beside the groom in front of a service table set in the middle of Church. Everyone stands. It is the Orthodox tradition to stand for worship. There are no pews or benches. It is not uncommon to have two, three or more priests celebrate the service, for every family has clerical relatives or

Chapter Seven: The Wedding

friends. The service is called "the crowning." Crowns, some elaborate and some simple, are among the sacral treasures of every Church. After the opening prayers, these crowns are given to the couple to kiss. Then, with an intricate flowing ritual, they are placed, blessed and exchanged three times on the heads of the couple. This crowning by God through the Church binds the couple in wedlock. Next, symbolizing their entrance on to the road of life, the priest leads the wedding party three times around the service table. A final prayer and benediction ends the relatively short ritual.

The unmarried friends of the bride and groom dance with the musicians outside the Church as they wait with the other guests for the newlyweds to emerge. Some women will scrutinize the way the couple comes out, divining from signs, such as who is the first over the threshold, who will rule the relationship. The musicians and the joyful crowd surround the new husband and wife as everybody moves off to the wedding feast. Whether the feast is in a home or the hall, upon arrival the couple is greeted by the cook and matron of the feast, standing at the top of the steps with a plate of grain. Casting the wheat from her plate, it is her honor to give the blessing from the hearth. The wheat carries the blessing of abundance, fertility and fecundity. Her charm may be rendered something like this:

"Wheat I throw, from off my plate
To bless this groom, here at the gate
More wheat I cast, from off my dish
To bless the bride, it is my wish
Bless this strong son, of our fair land
Bless this beauty, at his right hand
I throw this wheat, of fiery reds
To bring luck, upon their heads
Bless God, parents and family dear
Bless us all, from far and near."

Some see in the number of kernels caught in the bride's apron a count of the children she will bear. I have also witnessed at this point the ritual drinking together from a single goblet of wine. The wine is drunk. The glass is smashed. The symbol is clear. The elixir of wedding can only be drunk once in a life time. Once it is sipped it is forever passed. Like the glass that held it, it is shattered, destroyed and gone.

Weddings used to stretch out over three days. Now they run closer to twenty-four hours straight, with the feast consuming the larger portion. Stewards of the bottle keep the tables covered with drinks. Jovial gregarious older men move among the tables with tuica flasks, humorously intimidating hesitating guests into just one more toast to the newlyweds. The musicians circle through the cycle of dances. Stomping, spinning, jostling dancers crowd what little floor space is available. Waitresses move with agile nimbleness, balancing loaded plates out from the kitchen and dirty dishes back into it.

Chapter Seven: The Wedding

Smokers slowly fill the house or hall with a haze. Hours pass. Children fall asleep on the benches covered with their parents' coats. The arrival of the wedding cake in the wee hours long after midnight marks the end of the feasting. When the cake is finished it is time for the hen.

If the majestic ancient hymn of the Cherubim in the Divine Liturgy of the Church marks the mystical translation of those present into the heavenly realm, then in a reversed but similar way, the dance of the hen at the wedding feast marks the final translation of the sodden guests into an unabashed embrace of the earthly realm. The hen represents the bride. She is the bird offered up to be eaten. The ribald shouts and singing reflect the hushed-up realities of life. The roasted bird is laid out on a bed of greenery with a phallic cigarette in its beak. Her meat is bartered for. Every innuendo is used to suggest that she has been all around the barnyard. Amid uproarious explosions of laughter, vent is given to the seamy side of marriage, and sordid reality is neutralized with humor. Then, as far as the meat will go around, the hen is eaten by everyone; everyone that is, except the bride.

I have never made it beyond this point in a village wedding. The one time I witnessed the dance of the hen I had to wait up until 4:30 in the morning. Fortunately I managed to secret a bottle of mineral water under my seat and as soon as a toast was drunk, I deftly refilled my shot glass while no one was looking. Amidst my bleary-eyed table mates, I persevered rather nobly, but afterwards I was so exhausted that I still stumbled home just like them.

What happens at the end of a celebration is known to me only through books, conversations, and a videotape I once saw. A young man who had worked in Germany, had a camcorder and recorded a friend's wedding. In the film, I watched the newlyweds with a bedraggled cluster of wobbling young celebrants, sloshing unsurely behind the steadfast musicians, along a muddy road in the dim light of a late winter dawn. This wedding party went to the home of the new husband. There the married women sat the bride down in the center of the room, danced around her, removed her wedding crown that the maidens had placed on her, bound up her braids and tied a scarf around her head. Twice, according to custom, she tore the scarf from her head and threw it away. Only with the third attempt did it stay tied on. She was now a married woman. The last scenes of the video showed the groom, rather unsteadily, trying to dispatch his teasing buddies out into the now pouring rain so that he and his wife could be alone at last.

Chapter Eight: The Heart of the Village

Chapter Eight: The Heart of the Village

The interior world of the Orthodox villagers is similar to the interior of their Church. The Church walls are covered from floor to ceiling with colorfully painted icons. They are alive with images of biblical events, saints, sinners, demons and heavenly hosts. We may see them as only decorative or ornamental. To us the order may appear to be random or even chaotic. Yet, quite to the contrary, like the unseen world they represent, everything is strictly ordered. They reflect the events under-girding the existence of the world, they portray the calendar of the year, and they introduce in rank and order the inhabitants of the spiritual realm. To the initiated they are an open book. To the villager they map the geography of their inner life. Many a serious visitor to the village has been left uncomprehending because they didn't want to deal with the Church. Yet the Church is the key.

The icons are the map, but the services are the means. The Divine Liturgy is the central service of worship across the entire Orthodox world. It traces its roots to St. John Chrysostom, patriarch of Constantinople in the fourth century. In this service, somewhere near the mid-point, a moving hymn is sung. It is called the Cherubic Hymn. Liturgically, it marks the portal to the realm of holy mysteries. Through it the congregation ascends as they sing:

Chapter Eight: The Heart of the Village

"Let us who mystically represent the cherubim and who sing the thrice-holy hymn to the life-creating Trinity now lay aside all earthly cares."

And in laying aside all earthly cares the worshippers ascend to join the cherubim. Mystically they enter the ivory palaces of sacred space. Heaven and earth meld into one. The service continues in this holy realm. In the elements of bread and wine, Christ himself enters in the Chalice. The communion of saints assembles as the priest calls out across time to invite all the ancestors, fathers, patriarchs, prophets, apostles, preachers, evangelists, martyrs, confessors, ascetics and saints to join in. Then, as all the bells of the Church are set to ringing, the worship crests in a hymn to the Mother of God.

Mary, the Mother of God, may have all but evaporated out of the mainstream of Western Protestant Christianity, but in the ancient Churches of the East she still reigns with an exalted majesty that is at the same time humble, homey and approachable. Enter an Orthodox Church and your gaze will be drawn to her enormous icon dominating the space behind and above the altar. Facing the royal doors at the front and center of the Church, her icon will always be on the left-hand side, while that of her son is on the right. But find yourself anywhere among an Orthodox peasantry on August 15th and you will be caught up in a lavish

torrent of incredible devotion and worship. August 15th is the day on which the death of Mary is commemorated. Technically it is called the Feast of the Dormition, or the Feast of the Falling Asleep of the Mother of God. Among the villagers it is called, simply, Mary's Day. In practice and observance it is equaled only by Easter and Christmas.

As the feast day draws near, pilgrims start to wend their way toward a monastery. It is tradition to celebrate the feast at a monastery. In Romania there are hundreds of monasteries. They range from small compounds of a few monks or nuns to many communities numbering a hundred or more. Dormition services are seldom held in the village Churches. The local clergy join the assemblage at the monastery. There

they assist the monks in hearing confessions and ministering to the crowds. By August 14th the roads fill with pilgrims. In festive traditional dress, many walk for hours, covering countless miles. Individuals and clusters of pilgrims converge with groups from various villages, led by Church banners and children carrying icons, all singing their way to their chosen monastery. Women carry sacks of food for the communal cooking pots. Services begin with evening vespers, and as the light fades and evening cools, devotional services continue on through the night. Pilgrims camp in the fields around the open air altar of the monastery. By sunrise on the feast day itself, the roads clog with

Chapter Eight: The Heart of the Village

pilgrims as crowds swell into the thousands. Rural Romania comes to a halt for August 15th. Depending on the size and status of the monastery, a Bishop or some other Hierarch will celebrate the service attended by ranks of the local clergy.

As the Divine Liturgy crests in the glorious hymn to Mary, hundreds and often thousands kneel in adoration. In the icon of this feast the figure of Christ stands surrounded by the saints and apostles behind the laid out body of his mother, and to his bosom he takes a small white figure which is her soul. Consider this. As we have observed, the central devotional focus of the faith in the Eastern Orthodox tradition is not a cross or a crucifix, but an icon of Mary holding her son,

most often in an embrace of affection. Now in the icon of the Dormition the embrace is returned. The Son tenderly holds his mother's soul and carries her to the heavenly home. Mary ascends to the heavenly realm.

The subtleties and sophistries of a feminist fascination with a Goddess figure are lost on the women of the village. Try explaining the overtones of Goddess worship to an old world grandmother. All the village women know is that Mary is right up there with the Father, Son and Holy Ghost, and when you pray to her, she answers. That's all they know, all they want to know and all that really matters.

The ecclesiastical order of the Church may be patriarchal, and the social order of the village may be a

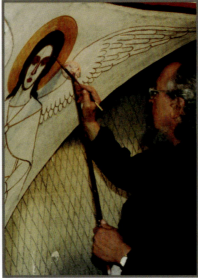

community, hawking their wares and creating an open-air market. I will never forget a little boy I once saw come running up to his sister, with his eyes large, round and excited. "What did you get for Mary's Day?" he asked, and before she could answer, he held out his treasures announcing; "Look! I got a rosary and a squirt gun!"

As the monasteries empty after the feast, the monastics return to their life of prayer. The old Orthodox world has never been empty of monasteries. These citadels of spirituality inspire and nurture the religious life of the land. Unlike many Western monastic orders that have developed service orientations, Orthodox monasteries have always been patriarchy, but with their hearts the believers grasp the power of the bond with the feminine. Over and over again in every Divine Liturgy, the blessing of the Mother of God is invoked. In the icon of the Dormition there is a diamond shaped background behind the figure of Christ holding the soul of Mary. In iconographic symbolism this signals that the truth portrayed is a mystery. It is truly a mystery. It is a mystery that approaches being an irony. Here in one of the most patriarchal of milieus, a woman and the feminine that she embodies, seem to be more profoundly understood, accepted, and revered, than in many a more overtly woman-friendly space.

During the feast day, itinerant merchants and peddlers set up shop on the fringe of the monastic

Chapter Eight: The Heart of the Village

or a man, in the Eastern tradition they are both simply called monastics. A youthful or romantic enthusiasm may entice a young person to enter the monastery. The age old custom of assigning tasks, or giving the novices what is called an obedience, soon pops any bubbles of illusion. Young boys and girls may try it for a few years and then decide that it is not for them. Those who continue, wrestle through their isolation from the normative social life of the outside world, and the assertion of their own inner biological drives. Often they will find a calling in the community. One will become a tailor, another an icon painter, a third will keep the cattle and another will assume the administration. It is from the ranks of the monks, all of whom are celibate, that most of the Bishops of the Church are elected. Some monastics become a bit peculiar from their struggles. When I am tempted to judge, I remember a

about the labor of prayer. They tend to withdraw from the world. They settle and build in hidden places, deep in the forest, high on the mountain, or lost in the desert. They are the keepers of the complex cycles of services dating back to the very dawn of Christian devotion. They are the guardians of the vast and rich treasure of the early centuries of the Church. Monasteries are places where the spiritual is palpable.

Monasteries may be spiritual but the monastics in them are human. Whether a woman

time when I was with a few friends, and we met an eccentric old monk in a Church. He was insisting on showing us how to make the sign of the cross. One of our group asked in English, so the old man couldn't understand, just what this crazy monk was thinking. I was stunned when another fellow answered the question with this wisdom: "I wouldn't be so quick to judge him crazy, for you have not heard his midnight prayers."

Obviously the devil throws his whole arsenal of temptations at the monastics. Some warp, but those who weather develop a sort of radiance. A lifetime ago a quiet country boy came to the Monastery of Sihistria with the request to become a monk. The abbot tested him, accepted him and sent him out to the mountainside meadows to tend the sheep. On the occasions when he came down to the monastery for services, the other monks were amused by his awkward reticent way. They viewed him as a dummy. As the story goes, eighteen

years passed and when the old abbot was on his death bed, he announced that this shepherd monk should be his successor. Unbelieving, a delegation set out to find the monk. The monk hid from them, relenting only when a high-ranking brother called out that this order to come down to the monastery was a matter of obedience. The dying abbot then presented the shepherd monk to the monastic community as their new abbot. To the astonishment of all, the one that they had called the dummy then spoke of his vision, revealing an awesome knowledge of the Church fathers and reflecting a profound

Chapter Eight: The Heart of the Village

piety. The old abbot knew of the shepherd's strength of soul and great learning, for he had been his confessor throughout the eighteen years of study and prayer while tending sheep on the high meadows. The shepherd monk, known to us as Father Cleopa, went on to lead the monastery through the years of communist oppression. By the time of his death, he was revered in all of Romania and much of the world for his spiritual counsel.

Such holy men and women, known as spiritual fathers and mothers, are a common and cherished fruit of the monasteries. The land is laced with them. To us from the western world of skepticism, it is hard to imagine such living saints. Yet they are there. They are loved and looked up to. I have met some of them and seen their cells with benches full of people waiting to confess or consult with them. Ask any villager and they will tell you tales of these holy ones that they have either met or heard about. Not only does the faith carry the believer heavenward, but those who have been hallowed by a life of prayer also bring down to us on earth a heavenly holiness.

However, not every monk or priest is such a holy soul. Most

are much more human. As individuals, the priests are as diverse as the villagers they serve. The majority tend their flock with something akin to the same diligence that the farmers exhibit in tending their fields and animals. The priesthood is an exhausting existence, and it is hard to remain reverent when the holy things are the commonplace elements of one's daily labor. Various men, energized by some passion for study or service, rise a little above simply doing their duty. A few wear out and become mechanical. Now and then one even finds a real scoundrel. Yet a dramatic dichotomy exists in the village between the priest as a person and the person as a priest. Almost magically, or superstitiously, when a man is ordained and receives the blessing to officiate at the holy rites, it no longer matters who he is; he becomes respected for what he is. He is the priest. When he walks the street the women stand and bow and the men tip their hats. He is greeted with the words: "Jesus be praised," and he answers, "forever amen."

The Church, like the priest and the village, exists on two levels. At one and the same time, it is this-worldly and other-worldly. It is a human institution with wealth, politics, intrigues and hierarchies, and at the same time it is the body of Christ, mystical, spiritual and sacramental. Anyone assuming that the Church is somehow different because it deals with the holy is in for a devastating disappointment. Church politics, especially in Orthodoxy, can be odious, vicious and vindictive. Yet at the same time, Orthodoxy especially,

Chapter Eight: The Heart of the Village

reaches and radiates a most sublime spirituality. The dung and muck of this world are a given in village life; therefore the striving for the sublime and beautiful is the life of the village.

Fasting precedes four of the feasts of the Church. All monastics and many devout souls fast on Wednesday and Friday. The great Lenten fast stretches out for 47 days before Easter. It is strictly observed, but after Easter it ends with the week in which fasting is equally as strictly forbidden. This is so typically Orthodox. The Church keeps the fasts, but it never seemed to develop the types of penitential discipline that evolved in some Western Christian lands. Perhaps the villagers were always so poor that they could never grasp how any more merit could be added to their soul by enduring yet more suffering. Instead, the Eastern Churches gave themselves more to embellishing their services of prayer and worship. Even the occasional discipline of a pilgrimage was not so much a matter of penance. It was more often undertaken to experience the beauty and blessing of some place like a great monastery at the end of the journey.

The Church calendar moves from feast to feast, and with it the villagers move from party to party. June 24th is the Feast of the Birth of John the Baptist, and the Church in the next village up the river is dedicated to his birth, so they will be celebrating their patronal feast. Your sister is married into that village so we will have

to go. The 29th is the Feast of Saints Peter and Paul. That's the Patronal Feast of the village behind us over the hill. We have to go. Of course there is Sunday in between and the 30th is the Feast of the Synaxsis of the Twelve Apostles which is the patronal celebration of the monastery at Barsana. Everybody is going to that. The Bishop is coming. So it goes. Massive kettles of cabbage rolls are cooked. Bottles of Tuica are consumed and daily drudgery is diverted by prayer, worship and genial gossiping.

Individual feasts are adorned with their own special customs. On January 6th there is the procession to the stream for the service of Blessing the Water. On Ascension Day there is the service of blessing the fields. However it is the high feasts of Christmas and Easter that manifest the full richness of the village soul. Christmas comes quietly for it is preceded by a fast. The fast isn't broken until after the liturgy of Christmas day, but the magic of the feast comes in the Holy Night before. All night long, singers in little clusters criss-cross the snow-covered villages and valleys, laying the sound of ancient carols to echo in the frozen air and haunt the soul. The Romanian poet, Stefan Hrusca, says this of these songs: "Romanian carols have a special metaphysical dimension which distinguishes them from the Christmas songs of all other peoples. Primeval sounds, primeval words, primeval rhythms: all these create—both for the singer and the listener—the cosmic image of Birth, Ascension and Purification by Faith."

Chapter Eight: The Heart of the Village

Christmas in the Romanian villages is these carols. Of course there is also the service in the Church, and the festive meal to break the fast (even if one didn't keep the fast). This is followed by the performance of the "Nativity Pageant." The presentation is called "The Bethlehem," and it is staged on a special platform built onto the outside front of the Church. It has its roots in the mystery play tradition of the medieval Church. It is a village honor to be allowed to play one of the parts. It follows roughly the Christmas story with the addition of some wild frightening fur-covered forest spirits who dash around, on and off stage, terrorizing the young boys and girls, much to the delight of the crowd. Every afternoon for the first three days of Christmas most of the villagers gather to watch the play. The priest, mayor and honored guests, sit on chairs at the back of the platform against the wall of the Church. Everyone seems to know the script, and each waits excitedly to react to the performance of their favorite parts. The audience is as much a part of the play as the actors, and essentially the same crowd returns day after day to enjoy the celebration.

The village year is the cycle of the Church calendar. The celebrations or feasts of the Church tell the stories that form the basis of village beliefs. They bind the people of the village together. The Church is simply the story teller that one finds at the heart of every culture. The Church tells the stories that teach the

Shadows of Yesterday

truths that the people believe in. At the same time, the people celebrate the truths that the stories teach. It is educational celebration and celebrative education. From Sunday to Sunday, from feast to feast, from year to year, using all the senses, the Church repeats the stories that are the foundation of the faith and the faithful celebrate the promises these stories proclaim.

The great culmination of this culture comes in the spring as the snow melts, the little creatures awaken, the meadows green, the lambs are born, the birds return and the trees flower. For six weeks the faithful abstain from meat and all dairy products. They observe hallowed rituals of devotion and pray special prayers. Then, for a final holy week, they keep a strict fast and attend services every day. For the first three days, they attend once a day and for the last four days, twice a day. In these days, according to elaborate ancient tradition, they re-enact with liturgical drama the events of the last days of the life of their Savior, Jesus the Christ. A tomb is built up in the center of the Church. Lavish displays of flowers decorate it and an icon of the body of Christ is carried in procession to it and laid out upon it. As in the Christmas play, so also in this Easter pageantry, everyone knows the story, the script and the services. Everyone waits for the special moments, the haunting hymns and the long lamentations.

Then, Saturday night at midnight, as an expectant congregation crowds into a completely darkened sanctuary, and often surrounds the outside of the Church as well, the cry rings forth: "Christ is risen!" Thunderously the believers respond: "He is risen indeed!" The bells are set to pealing. The cry is repeated. The response thunders back. The priest emerges from the royal doors holding aloft a single candle. The light spreads to the candles held

Chapter Eight: The Heart of the Village

by everyone in the congregation. The choir takes up the resurrection hymn. The priest cries out "Christ is risen!" in every language that he knows. The response "He is risen indeed!" thunders in a cacophony of languages. Anyone who has not witnessed an Orthodox Easter service, especially in a village, cannot imagine it. These were the experiences that seared the faith into the soul of our immigrant ancestors.

The dawn of Easter day seeps out of the darkness just as it does everyday. Slowly it crawls into the morning mists and the earth reawakens. Man yawns, stretches, pulls on his clothes and stumbles out to the labors of his day. The cow needs milking, the animals need feeding, and the barn needs emptying. It is just like it always was. The woman rattles the grates, kindles the fire and prepares to cook breakfast. It is just like it always was. Then the muffled tone of the Church bell echoes in the fog. Faith awakens. It is not just like it always was. He is risen. Life goes on. That's the message. That's the faith. That makes all the difference in the world. Slowly the sun slides through the morning mists cutting the chill. Warmth returns.

Shadows of Yesterday

About the Author

Outwardly, Alvin Alexsi Currier is known as a son of the city of Minneapolis, born there in 1932, and until his retirement in 1990 after 35 years, he was known professionally as a Presbyterian clergyman who served various Midwestern American Churches, two parishes in Germany and for 11 years as a college chaplain.

Inwardly he is a pilgrim who, sensing his spiritual emptiness, fled professional life for the forest in 1975. There over the next two decades he lived a semi-monastic life, founding and tending St. Herman's Hermitage as a place of prayer for all people. In 1991 he was received along with his wife Anastasia, into the Orthodox Church of America.

Living eleven years without electricity awakened his sensitivity to the potency of living intimately with creation, and he began traveling as much as possible, to study through experience, still extant peasant cultures. As an artist and author he is known for his book on Orthodox Karelia, his children's books, his collection of Ritual Towels and his regular pilgrimages to the inside of Eastern Orthodox Europe.

In an ever active retirement, he and his wife now have their home in Ajijic, Mexico. He may be contacted at a.currier@juno.com